# OVERVIEW

**Overview**

Strict hierarchical authority structures are becoming less common in the workplace. Instead, companies are more laterally organized, with a focus on collaborative teamwork. So good influencing skills are more important than ever for success in the workplace.

Cultivating cooperative relationships and building credibility are the foundations on which you can build influence and so get the results you need. Influencing skills are essential no matter what your position – but they're especially important if you don't have direct authority over those you need help from.

In this book, you'll learn to build relationships and credibility by gaining an understanding of these issues:
- the importance and characteristics of influence, and the benefits of having good influencing skills,
- how to cultivate positive, cooperative relationships at work so you have the ability to influence others, and

- how to build your credibility at work, so others recognize you as a person of integrity.

To get what you want in a situation where you have no authority, you need to communicate persuasively.

You need to use oral communication properly if you want to be taken seriously and be seen as credible. This is especially true when you don't have authority. It then becomes critical that you communicate well – as well as persuasively – otherwise it's likely you won't get what you set out to achieve.

Consider sales calls and telesales. The salespeople must have effective communication skills. Because they have only a limited time to sell their product, they must be highly persuasive speakers.

You may not be a salesperson, but you still need to be able to influence your colleagues, whether you're asking for a simple favor, a major commitment, or a buy-in for your ideas. Without formal authority, you can't simply order people to do your bidding. Persuasive communication can help.

Sometimes, even if you have prepared to the best of your ability, you may still meet some resistance. Knowing how to communicate persuasively involves knowing how to overcome resistance so you can achieve the result you want.

In this book, you'll learn more about the following strategies of persuasive communication:
- how to use persuasive communication and why it is key in getting the results you want,
- how to apply the strategies for communicating persuasively in a realistic situation, and

- how to overcome resistance to getting what you want.

In economics, the "no free lunch" rule encapsulates the idea that to get something you want, you need to give something back. Or if you give nothing, you get nothing.

In its simplest sense, the idea of exchange is illustrated when you go to a store and exchange money for a desired item.

This idea of exchange – also known as "reciprocity" or "give-and-take" – isn't restricted to material items. It's a universal principle that applies to all kinds of situations.

Reciprocity becomes especially pertinent in cases where you need to influence people you have no direct authority over.

You may need help from a colleague on a project, for example. Or you may need key information from someone in order to complete an important report.

Reciprocity can be either positive or negative.

**Positive**

In positive reciprocity, the exchanges are mutually beneficial. For example, "If you cover my weekend shift this Saturday, I'll cover yours next month."

**Negative**

In negative reciprocity, the exchanges are negative or threatening. For example, "If you don't come to this meeting, you won't receive a production bonus."

You should avoid a negative bias in exchanges unless it's necessary. Negative bias can create a pattern of hostility – which can be very counter-productive in a work environment. Negative bias can also build mistrust and damage perceptions of individuals in the organization.

Instead, try to have a positive bias in exchanges, as this creates win-win situations and is more conducive to healthy and productive long-term work relationships.

In this book, you'll learn how to be reciprocal:
- develop an effective give-and-take strategy,
- identify different objects of trade, and
- recognize how to use different trading approaches.

Knowing how to make trades effectively will help you influence those over whom you have no authority. This influence can help you to get the results you need, making your work more effective.

Consider you and your boss's relationship. Are you able to make a request to take on more responsibility? Can you get the direction you need? Are you happy with the relationship you have with your boss – with how you and your boss work together? If you have answered no to any of these questions, you may need to build influence with your boss in order to improve your situation.

Building influence with your boss can have many benefits. If you have influence, your boss is far more likely to listen to your thoughts and ideas.

You may be given more latitude, more support, or more challenging assignments. The key is to gain influence with your boss in a way that builds your relationship rather than threatens it.

If you view your relationship with your boss as a partnership, you focus on cooperating and learning from each other. It's a give-and-take relationship that can be different from that in the traditional superior-subordinate relationship.

### Getting Results without Direct Authority

It enables you to have influence because in such a partnership you understand the interests, needs, and objectives of your boss, know what you have that is valuable to your boss, and interact in a style you know that your boss prefers.

In this book, you'll learn about these strategies that will help you be influential with your boss, so you can get the results you want at work:
- understand your boss's situation,
- know what you can offer your boss to help achieve both your goals, and
- use an appropriate style with your boss to get what you need.

You'll also find out how to how to influence your boss to give you more responsibility or direction.

# CHAPTER 1 - BUILDING RELATIONSHIPS AND CREDIBILITY

## CHAPTER 1 - Building Relationships and Credibility
Section 1 - Influencing Others to Get Results
Section 2 - Cultivating Relationships to Get Results
Section 3 - Building Credibility to Get Results

# SECTION 1 - INFLUENCING OTHERS TO GET RESULTS

**Section 1 - Influencing Others to Get Results**

Having the ability to influence others is essential, especially when you lack formal authority. Influencing others requires that you identify interests you share with other people and use these in persuading them to support mutually beneficial ideas or courses of action.

Having strong influencing skills can enable you to complete work more efficiently, reduce conflict and the stress it generates, demonstrate that you're a team player, and be a better negotiator.

# IMPORTANCE OF INFLUENCING SKILLS

**Importance of influencing skills**

In the workplace, being able to influence others is critical, particularly when you don't have clear authority. For example, you may need to influence someone in another department to help you finish an important project. Your success, and even your ability to complete your own work, can depend on how good you are at persuading others to help you.

Consider Angela who is a product designer. She's working on a new line of children's toys and needs to get the cooperation of a key person in marketing to test out one of the products she's developing. She calls marketing a few times to make her request, but she doesn't get anywhere. She can't move forward until she knows the design is workable. A colleague's project moves ahead of hers and she's worried her design will lose priority.

If Angela had managed to convince marketing of the importance of the project, they might have responded.

**Question**

### Getting Results without Direct Authority

How do you think Angela could influence the key person in the Marketing Department to help her?

**Options:**

1. Show marketing the benefits of helping with the product
2. Determine something you can offer marketing in return for help
3. Give clear directions to ensure compliance
4. Take a forceful approach and give a direct order

**Answer**

Option 1: This is a correct option. If Angela shows marketing how they would benefit from helping her, she'll be more influential. When you consider another person's perspective, you become more influential. For example, marketing might like to be acknowledged as part of the team that brings out a groundbreaking product.

Option 2: This option is correct. Influence can sometimes be about give and take. If Angela indicates she can help marketing in some way, they may respond to her request. For example, she can suggest a way to get key information to marketing quicker, particularly if this has been an issue between marketing and product development.

Option 3: This option is incorrect. It's important to give clear directions, but this may not influence the other party to spend time helping out. You need more than clarity to be influential.

Option 4: This is an incorrect option. Taking a forceful approach could make marketing even less likely to help. You might antagonize a crucial peer or superior. This can easily come back to haunt you.

Because strict hierarchical structures are becoming less common in the workplace, a need for good influencing skills exists.

If you have effective influencing skills, you'll have the edge you need to get what you want and build more productive business relationships.

But how exactly do you influence others? Is it a form of manipulation?

There's a big difference between influencing others and manipulating them. Influencing means you focus not only on getting what you need or want, but on improving your relationship with others. You're truthful about your objectives, but also aware your colleagues have their own goals. You remain flexible. Manipulation is about using a relationship only to get what you want. It means you have little or no consideration of the impact on the other person.

Influencing others involves a certain amount of give and take. Bargaining and making exchanges are so much a part of human interaction that often you don't realize these processes are happening. But most of our relationships, including those at work, enact the "law of reciprocity." This means colleagues expect to be paid back for what they do. Do you expect that those you have done something for "owe you" and will repay you in some way? Chances are you do.

**Reciprocal relationships**

If you cultivate reciprocal relationships with others by supporting their interests, they'll return the favor and support you when the time comes. For example, you may help a colleague finish an important report. You implicitly expect that when the circumstance is right, she'll do something of approximately equal value for you. Later, you may think of her when you need an extra hand on an important project.

How would you characterize a good influencer? Some common traits are that good influencers approach others as equals, they quickly identify common ground, and they are generally well liked.

**Approach others as equals**

When good influencers approach others, they don't think about differences in power and authority. This is easy when the person you're dealing with is a peer or has less power than you. But it's typically a challenge when the person has more authority than you.

In such a case, you have to rely on the strength of your ideas, the value of what you're doing, or your reputation or expertise.

**Quickly identify common ground**

Good influencers quickly identify common ground and shared interests, usually through skillful questioning and listening.

Although it may seem you have opposing views or conflicting priorities with the person you approach, you can usually reframe your position to make it clear that you both share interests – for example, your organization's goals.

**Are generally well liked**

Typically, good influencers understand that professional interactions involve exchanges. They're friendly, helpful, and willing to cooperate with the reasonable requests of others. So they're well liked and able to call in favors when they need to. And others are happy to help in return.

# BENEFITS OF INFLUENCING SKILLS

**Benefits of influencing skills**

There's no doubt that possessing influencing skills has benefits. It can help you get your work done faster, reduce conflict and stress, and demonstrate that you're a team player. And if you're good at influencing others, you'll also be a better negotiator – a key skill in and outside the workplace.

Few people are able to do their jobs in isolation. You may rely on the results of your colleagues' work or on information they provide. Or you might rely on them to follow through after you've finished your part of a task.

So how quickly you get work done depends partly on how well others meet your requirements. If you have good influencing skills, it's easier to get what you need to complete your work, when you need it.

What do you think would be the result if you kept your head down, working only in your immediate area? You wouldn't last too long. Interdependence is a key characteristic of the workplace. Typically, you'll be dependent on, and important to, a variety of colleagues.

Successfully influencing your colleagues to give you what you need requires that you identify shared interests. This means you need to make sure your colleagues know how fulfilling your request will benefit them.

Carrie works in the Human Resources Department. She feels it's vital to improve employee morale, but senior managers don't believe investing time and resources in this is a priority.

So when Carrie presents her ideas, she focuses on proving how the company will ultimately lower staff turnover, save money currently spent on training new staff, and improve productivity.

Instead of focusing only on the benefits for employees or for her department, Carrie identifies shared interests and uses these to win over senior managers.

Some conflict is inevitable in the workplace. For example, when your ideas or interests differ with those of others, all parties may simply argue their own views. With good influencing skills, you can reduce this conflict and the stress it generates. You can eliminate resistance and convince colleagues you don't know to help you.

**Eliminate resistance**

As a good influencer, you don't react to resistance by becoming more aggressive or forceful. You know this reaction causes conflict and stress for everyone.

If you know others are likely to be resistant to a particular idea, it's important to frame this idea as a solution to a mutual problem – or to outline the benefits it could have for everyone.

By identifying this common ground quickly, you reduce the potential for conflict. You also stop others from developing mental blocks against your suggestions.

## Convince colleagues to help you

It can be difficult to ask colleagues you don't know well to complete tasks that require a lot of time and energy. You need to do some research before you approach them to prevent conflict and undue stress on yourself. For example, if you don't do your research, you may suggest something that your colleague refuses outright. As a result, you may develop a negative view of this individual.

A good influencer avoids this by finding out what the other side is interested in. By doing this, you'll be able to clarify how fulfilling your request benefits the other party and you'll be able to offer an appropriate exchange.

Good influencers are typically well liked. That's because they recognize the needs and interests of others. And they're able to communicate their requests in a way that's attractive to the other party. This goes a long way in helping to avoid conflicts with others.

For example, some people assume their colleagues will interpret things their way and quickly agree to a request. They therefore communicate the request somewhat abruptly because they're assuming their colleagues understand the importance.

Good influencers know how to avoid this situation by finding out what is of interest to the other party and offering something appropriate to get a positive response.

Because influencing others involves taking their interests into account, you can demonstrate you're a team player – a cooperative person who's willing to give as well as take. This is important in a workplace of interdependent relationships. Your relationships with colleagues matter – the better your relationships, the more chance you have of being able to influence others. You'll be able to find the right people to trade with and build up goodwill to help the trades along.

You can ask for a favor in different ways – some of which will get you what you want, while others won't.

**Corbin**

"Hi. Listen, I really need you to take over a client I have coming in at 3:00 p.m. I have this report to write for the new managing director and it's really important I get it finished before the end of the day. Can you help?"

**Gabriel**

"Good morning. May I ask you something? The new managing director wants me to finish a report, which I think will help our team get those extra resources it needs. The problem is, I won't have time to finish it if I meet my 3:00 p.m. client. I know you're really busy too, but would you be able to take over that meeting for me? I can make it up to you later by helping you with your research."

Although Corbin and Gabriel are asking for the same favor, you're probably less inclined to help Corbin. He focuses only on what he needs and why it's important to him.

Gabriel, however, approaches you as an equal and acknowledges your priorities. He proves he's a team player by focusing on how his request will benefit the team as a whole and by offering to help you meet your own targets.

Because Gabriel shows he's a team player, you'd probably be happy to help him again in future or to ask for his help when you need it. Your professional relationship is likely to be more reciprocal and cooperative.

In addition to being seen as a team player, getting work done faster and reducing conflict and stress, good influencing skills can help you when you're engaged in negotiations. Negotiating is an important skill in business. You need it to maintain cooperative relationships with those you work with, to make win-win trades, and to meet your professional goals.

Negotiating is about finding a mutually beneficial solution or deal. So it follows that the skills of a good influencer apply in negotiations.

For example, being able to establish common ground and shared interests is important in finding win-win trades in negotiations.

Moreover, good influencers are usually well liked. This can only help when you have to negotiate with others. A good influencer has likely built a reputation for offering exchanges that are mutually beneficial.

Latitia is a project manager for a large publishing house. She wants the green light for a community project involving the distribution of textbooks to secondary schools.

In her negotiations with senior managers, she points out what the project could do for the company's image. She offers to provide the Marketing Department with whatever material it needs to advertise the company's community involvement. And after some bargaining, her project is approved.

Because of Latitia's ability to identify her managers' interests and to offer a trade, she's able to negotiate a win-win situation.

**Question**

## Getting Results without Direct Authority

What benefits are you likely to realize if you have strong skills in influencing others?

**Options:**

1. You'll work more efficiently

2. You'll be able to overcome resistance to your ideas without causing conflict

3. You'll be able to demonstrate you're a cooperative person

4. You'll be able to make more effective win-win trades in business negotiations

5. You'll be able to get people to do things for you without having to do anything for them

6. You'll be able to get people to put aside their own goals for the sake of your personal success

**Answer**

Option 1: This is a correct option. Because people are more likely to agree to your requests if you have strong influencing skills, you're likely to get work done faster and more efficiently.

Option 2: This option is correct. With strong influencing skills, you identify common ground with others – even if they're initially resistant to your ideas. Instead of taking offense to their resistance, which can lead to conflict, you find ways to persuade the other party of the benefits to them of helping you out.

Option 3: This is a correct option. If you have good influencing skills, you're able to show people you're a team player who's willing to cooperate with others. In turn, others will be more willing to cooperate with you.

Option 4: This option is correct. Having good influencing skills makes you a better negotiator, who's able to identify both parties' interests and work toward finding a mutually satisfying solution.

Option 5: This option is incorrect. Having good influencing skills involves applying the principles of give and take, in reciprocal, cooperative relationships.

Option 6: This is an incorrect option. Influencing others isn't the same as manipulating them for personal gain. Rather, it involves finding win-win solutions.

# SECTION 2 - CULTIVATING RELATIONSHIPS TO GET RESULTS

**Section 2 - Cultivating Relationships to Get Results**

To exert influence in the workplace even if you lack formal authority, you need to develop strong, positive relationships with your colleagues and managers. You can do this over time by consistently taking an interest in others, being respectful, and being positive.

To demonstrate that you take an interest in others, it's important to listen carefully and to be open to their ideas and feedback. You should practice putting yourself in other people's shoes and, when appropriate, ask for or offer help so that you can find out more about them.

Being respectful involves treating others as your peers – remaining polite and showing consideration for their needs – and showing appreciation for their work. People who feel you respect them are more likely to cooperate with you.

To remain positive, you should be generally cheerful, emphasize the good points about situations and people's work, and offer support when it's needed. Positive people tend to have more influence than those who are negative.

# RELATIONSHIPS AND INFLUENCE

**Relationships and influence**

At work, your relationships with others help determine the level of influence you have. It's natural that if you have good relationships with colleagues and managers, they'll be more likely to support your ideas and comply with your requests. But how do you go about cultivating these relationships?

You can think about it this way. How inclined are you to go out of your way to support the ideas of someone who tends to be grumpy, unhelpful, and unappreciative? What about someone who has helped you out in the past and is always a pleasure to work with?

It makes sense you're more likely to find value in the ideas put forward by a colleague you like and respect.

Similarly, you'll cultivate better work relationships and get more support if your coworkers like working with you and you make them feel valued. When this is the case, you're more likely to get the results you want or need from others even if you lack formal authority.

You can develop strong work relationships in many different ways. Typically, though, any approach will require that you take these steps:
- show interest in others, asking about and paying attention to their concerns,
- be respectful to your coworkers and managers, treating them as you'd like to be treated yourself, and
- be positive, remaining optimistic and offering others support when it's needed.

# SHOWING INTEREST IN OTHERS

**Showing interest in others**

You can show interest in the people you interact with at work in a variety of ways. For example, ask questions and listen carefully to the answers. Put yourself in your coworkers' shoes to uncover their needs and interests. And ask for or offer help whenever this is appropriate.

**Ask questions and listen to the answers**

You can show interest in your colleagues by regularly asking them about their concerns. For instance, ask what they're currently working on and about any challenges or difficulties they're experiencing. Also ask how they feel about particular situations.

Then ensure you listen attentively to the responses. Give a colleague who's responding to a question your full attention and make it clear you're interested and empathetic.

**Put yourself in coworkers' shoes**

To understand your colleagues – how they view situations and how they behave – you need to put yourself in their shoes. Consider their perspectives and imagine how you'd think or feel from their points of view. You should also consider their personal preferences and work styles.

This will help you identify what's important to your colleagues. In turn, you'll have a better understanding of the factors likely to motivate them to support ideas you put forward.

**Ask for or offer help**

Offering colleagues help with their tasks is a good way to get to know them better and to earn their respect and support.

Similarly, asking others for help can strengthen your relationships – it shows you appreciate their input and enables you to work together, sharing your expertise and experiences. This can enrich the relationships you have.

Nick has a new idea for improving communication at his workplace. He needs to win support from his colleagues if the idea is to be put into practice.

The first thing Nick does is to set aside time to meet with his colleagues to ask how they feel about the current communication system. When they tell him what they think, Nick gives them his full attention. He also responds to what they say, nodding in agreement or asking further questions when relevant.

For example, one of his colleagues complains that not everyone knows how to use the current system, which is complex. Nick takes this into account and decides to include a simple training scheme for his new communication system. This shows his coworkers he's sincerely interested in what they think.

Next, before pitching his idea, Nick puts himself in his colleagues' shoes. He thinks about their work styles, about the tasks they're responsible for completing, and about the sorts of deadline pressures they face.

For example, one of his colleagues, Sarah, has to meet tight deadlines on a regular basis. She's known for her ability to collate data rapidly and make snappy decisions – but waiting for information from others can slow her down.

Putting himself in his colleagues' shoes helps Nick determine how his idea could benefit each of his colleagues personally. He can incorporate this information when presenting his idea, making it more likely he'll win support for it. For example, he could make it clear to Sarah that the new system he's proposing will ensure she gets the information she needs much faster.

Finally, Nick decides to ask some of his colleagues how they think the current communication system could be simplified. This shows he values their insights. It also gives Nick a chance to work with them, building mutual respect and stronger relationships.

When Nick does pitch his idea, his colleagues identify the benefits right way. That's because Nick has taken the time to incorporate their interests and needs.

So by showing interest in his colleagues in various ways, Nick has substantially increased his level of influence.

**Question**

Steve has an idea for a new advertising campaign and hopes Gwen, his coworker, will agree with him.

How can Steve show interest in Gwen as he interacts with her?

**Options:**

1. Ask Gwen what ideas she has and listen carefully to her responses, before explaining his idea

2. Recognize Gwen's priorities as the person responsible for managing the marketing budget and refer to these when explaining his idea

3. Offer to help Gwen develop a proposal for her client

4. Laugh especially loudly whenever Gwen makes a joke

5. Ask for her comments after asserting the importance of his idea

**Answer**

Option 1: This option is correct. Asking questions and listening carefully to the responses is an important way of showing interest in someone. If Gwen feels Steve is interested in her and her ideas, she's more likely to be influenced by him.

Option 2: This is a correct option. By determining Gwen's interests and priorities, Steve is putting himself in her shoes. This is an effective way of showing interest in her – and is likely to make her more supportive of his idea.

Option 3: This option is correct. Offering colleagues your help is a way to demonstrate interest in their needs. Gwen's more likely to support Steve if she feels their relationship is a reciprocal one, in which she also obtains support from him.

Option 4: This is an incorrect option. Gwen is likely to recognize behavior like this as manipulative and fake. It doesn't involve demonstrating real interest in her or her concerns.

Option 5: This option is incorrect. If Steve is overly assertive and doesn't initially show that he values Gwen's interests and ideas, he's less likely to succeed in winning her support.

# BEING RESPECTFUL

**Being respectful**
As well as showing interest in your coworkers, it's important always to be respectful. If you treat others courteously and with respect, they're more likely to cooperate with and support you. Conversely, failing to show others respect is a sure way to discourage them from helping you.

You can show respect by treating others as you'd like to be treated yourself. Always be polite and consider others' feelings and needs. This can sometimes be difficult to remember when you're caught up in your own work and in getting your own needs met.

But try to listen to and encourage your colleagues. For example, don't interrupt someone who's presenting an idea by pointing out flaws in this person's thinking.

Instead listen actively to ensure you fully understand and show you recognize the value of this person's contribution. Once you've done this, you can state your opinions or thoughts in a constructive way, without putting the other person down.

It's important to be sincere in the respect you show others. Behaving respectfully shouldn't involve a conscious attempt to get them to do what you want. This is manipulative and dishonest, and likely to be picked up as fake.

So instead of treating colleagues as "targets" whose support you need to win, treat them as peers who naturally deserve your respect.

Showing appreciation for the efforts of others is a further aspect of showing respect. When your colleagues feel appreciated, they'll be more motivated – and more willing to go the extra mile on your behalf. You can show appreciation simply by remembering to say 'thank you" and to compliment good work.

**Say "thank you"**

It's easy to overlook the importance of saying "thank you" in the workplace, especially if someone regularly gives you information or completes tasks on your behalf. The simple act of thanking someone makes it clear you've recognized their efforts.

If you don't say "thank you" to someone who's helped you, this person is less likely to put in extra effort on your behalf in the future.

**Compliment good work**

People like to be recognized for doing good work. In fact, failing to recognize others' achievements can leave them discouraged.

When colleagues complete tasks well, particularly if it's something they helped you with, it's important to compliment their work. They're likely to remember your positive response and this will increase your influence when you make future requests for their help.

### Question

Daniel is a fairly new employee. He's had an idea of a new approach he thinks could save his team time and effort. If he wants his coworkers to take his idea seriously, he needs to demonstrate that he respects them.

In which ways can Daniel do this?

### Options:

1. Consider his coworkers' views and ideas, and be encouraging

2. Thank his coworkers whenever they provide him with information or advice

3. Compliment coworkers for the quality of their work, whenever warranted

4. Always be truthful with coworkers about their ideas, immediately pointing out any flaws or ways they can be improved

5. Assert control over his coworkers so they respect him more

### Answer

Option 1: This option is correct. An important way to demonstrate respect for others is to be aware of their concerns and needs. If Daniel's coworkers feel he's interested in and supportive of them, they're likely to respond in kind when Daniel has an idea to present.

Option 2: This is a correct option. Simply saying "thank you" shows respect. This will make Daniel's coworkers feel appreciated, and more ready to listen to and support his ideas.

Option 3: This option is correct. If Daniel makes his coworkers feel appreciated for their efforts, they're more likely to be receptive to his ideas.

Option 4: This is an incorrect option. Although Daniel should be honest, he won't earn support by criticizing the ideas of others. Instead he should focus on showing appreciation of his coworkers' efforts, offering constructive criticism only if he's asked to and in a supportive way.

Option 5: This option is incorrect. If Daniel attempts to assert authority he hasn't earned or doesn't have through formal channels, his coworkers are unlikely to be supportive. He may be identified as pushy, and others will be less likely to hear him out or take his ideas seriously.

# BEING POSITIVE

**Being positive**

As well as showing interest in others and being respectful, being positive can strengthen your work relationships. Being positive means you should be cheerful as much as possible and focus on the good in situations rather than dwelling on what's bad. It also means you give others your support by encouraging or assisting them in their efforts.

**Be cheerful**

Being cheerful and optimistic can lighten the mood of those around you and encourage them to do their best, even when challenges arise.

Also, it's easier to develop a relationship with someone who's generally friendly and cheerful than with someone who's always neutral or pessimistic. People are drawn to those who are cheerful.

**Focus on what's good**

By focusing on what's good in a situation or in work completed by others, you're more likely to earn their cooperation.

If you have only negative things to say, it's often worth staying quiet, or it may leave others feeling resentful and discouraged. Or emphasizing the positive before delivering negative feedback can make people more receptive. Similarly, focusing on the good after a setback or failure can motivate others and help them persevere.

**Give others support**

Supporting your colleagues and those around is an important aspect of remaining positive. Encourage their efforts and offer assistance when you can.

If you notice one of your colleagues struggling, you may also offer your support confidentially. This will strengthen your relationship, and is likely to win you a future ally.

As well as maintaining a generally positive demeanor, it's vital to avoid specific types of negative behavior. Even if you're usually optimistic and supportive, nothing wrecks a good relationship more quickly than an offensive or belittling remark. So to develop both your work relationships and your influence, it's important to watch your behavior and ensure you remain positive.

**Question**

You work as part of a team in the Marketing Department of a large company. You know that being positive will help encourage your coworkers – and make it more likely that they'll support your proposals for marketing campaigns.

What can you do to remain positive?

**Options:**

1. Encourage your colleagues and offer them your help when challenges arise

2. Always emphasize the positive elements of your colleagues' marketing proposals before offering constructive criticism

3. Maintain a cheerful disposition in the office

4. Keep the mood light by teasing your coworkers about their ideas

5. Ensure you point out all the benefits associated with your proposals and explain how they overcome problems in your colleagues' proposals

**Answer**

Option 1: This is a correct option. By offering your encouragement and support, you demonstrate a positive approach – and make it more likely that colleagues will support you in turn.

Option 2: This option is correct. It's important you avoid focusing on the negative. Even when it's necessary to disagree or point out possible flaws, it's best to begin by noting what's positive in colleagues' work or ideas.

Option 3: This is a correct option. If you're generally cheerful and optimistic, others will find it easier to get along with you – and they'll be more likely to support your ideas. Conversely, negativity can rub off on people you interact with, making them less open to your influence and less supportive.

Option 4: This option is incorrect. Being negative about others' ideas, even in a joking fashion, can be hurtful – and it makes it much less likely that others will be open to your ideas. It shows a lack of respect as well.

Option 5: This is an incorrect option. Influencing others does involve persuading them of the benefits of your ideas. However, aggressively promoting your own

Sorin Dumitrascu

ideas while criticizing those of others is unlikely to win you support.

# SECTION 3 - BUILDING CREDIBILITY TO GET RESULTS

**Section 3 - Building Credibility to Get Results**

An important way to increase the influence you have is to build your credibility in the workplace.

Over time, you can do this by ensuring you always honor the confidentiality of information trusted to you, deliver on your promises, accept responsibility for your work – including your mistakes – and acknowledge the contributions of others, and strengthen your expertise.

# BUILDING CREDIBILITY

**Building credibility**

Having influence over others requires that you have credibility. Consider someone who regularly lets you down. This person doesn't get back to you when promised and has given you unreliable information in the past. How likely are you to be open to this person's ideas?

The amount of influence you have over others depends on how they perceive you.

For example, are you seen as someone credible whose input they can trust?

And are you regarded as a person of integrity?

Your credibility is the extent to which others feel you can be trusted and believed. It isn't something you can turn on with the flick of a switch – it must be built over time.

Being perceived as credible will give weight to your opinions and decisions, even if you lack formal authority.

**Question**

How would you rate your level of credibility in the workplace?

### Getting Results without Direct Authority

**Options:**
1. High
2. Medium
3. Low

**Answer**

Option 1: You indicate that your credibility is high. This means your managers and colleagues trust you and may turn to you for help. You have likely built this level of credibility over time perhaps by being consistent in delivering on your promises, by accepting responsibility for your actions, and by demonstrating expertise in a certain area.

Option 2: You indicate that your credibility is medium. This may mean you need to spend some time building more credibility with your managers and colleagues. It takes time to do this, but you can take action - for example by honoring confidentiality, delivering on your promises, and accepting responsibility.

Option 3: You indicate that your credibility is low. You need to spend some time to develop it. If you want to be influential in situations where you don't have direct authority, managers and colleagues need to regard you as a credible person. There are actions you can take to help build your credibility - for example you could deliver on your promises, accept responsibility, and strengthen your expertise.

You can build your credibility over time in four main ways. You should honor confidentiality to earn your managers and colleagues' trust, always deliver on your promises, accept responsibility for your actions, and strengthen your expertise to gain trust on a professional level.

**Honor confidentiality**

Proving you can honor confidences by not revealing them develops people's trust in you and makes them feel like they can entrust you with information.

**Deliver on your promises**

Following through on your promises is vital if you want to appear credible to your colleagues. Someone who makes idle promises won't earn trust from anyone.

**Accept responsibility**

Accepting responsibility for your actions – including your mistakes – and giving others credit where it's due are important techniques if you want others to trust you.

**Strengthen your expertise**

Your professional credibility – and therefore your level of influence – depends on your expertise. If you know your field and research your ideas carefully, your opinions will carry more weight with others.

# HONORING CONFIDENTIALITY

**Honoring confidentiality**

When colleagues share private or potentially sensitive information with you, they trust you. Revealing the information to others breaks this trust – and lets them know you might not protect their confidences either. So consistently honoring the confidentiality of sensitive information is an important step when you develop a trustworthy reputation.

If you honor the need for confidentiality whenever it's appropriate to do this, it shows you care about others and are willing to protect their interests.

In business, those in positions of authority have access to confidential information. Managers and important decision makers will naturally value employees whom they know they can trust. Similarly, colleagues are more likely to pass on the information they have if they know they can trust you with it.

So if you're good at keeping confidences, it's also likely your managers and colleagues will give you more access to information. And because you're more informed, they'll give more weight to your opinions and you'll have increased influence over others.

Protecting confidentiality in the workplace goes beyond just knowing when to keep quiet. As well as keeping verbal communication private, it involves ensuring the privacy of written or printed documents, and of electronic data. So you make sure you don't leave photocopies unattended at the copy machine and you use passwords to protect electronic information.

Take the example of Joseph, who's a lead copywriter for a large advertising agency. He's often called on to work on multiple projects for different clients and is privy to sensitive information about these clients.

Often campaign ideas developed by a project team in conjunction with one client could be put to good use by teams working for other clients – and doing this would cut down on the time Joseph has to invest in each project.

However, Joseph doesn't discuss the details of any project, either with potential new clients or with the internal teams working on other projects.

Joseph's actions help him and his company maintain the trust of existing clients – who are then more likely to become repeat customers.

Joseph also develops a reputation for being trustworthy among his colleagues and the managers of each of the project teams. They feel safe divulging sensitive information to him because they know he won't repeat it to others.

Despite his lack of seniority, his coworkers all value his opinions. So his integrity translates into greater influence in the workplace.

**Question**

### Getting Results without Direct Authority

How can you honor confidentiality and therefore gain influence in your workplace?

**Options:**

1. Don't reveal sensitive information from a colleague who's asked you to keep it private

2. Let your manager know about information a peer shared with you in confidence

3. Password protect a design idea that your manager's shared with you in confidence

4. Share information you find on a report left at the copy machine

**Answer**

Option 1: This option is correct. By not revealing the information your colleague has told you, you're honoring confidentiality.

Option 2: This is an incorrect option. Even if you share confidential information with a manager or someone who is more senior than you, you're still betraying someone's trust.

Option 3: This is a correct option. You should take all precautions to protect confidential information, including encoding data and locking up printed documents.

Option 4: This is an incorrect option. Even if nobody's asked you to keep information confidential, you should assume it was left there by mistake. You should try to locate and return the documents to the owner.

# DELIVERING ON YOUR PROMISES

**Delivering on your promises**

How often have you chosen a product or service because of its proven track record? Nothing beats reliability when it comes to establishing a reputation, and this goes for business and personal relationships too. Just as people trust those who honor confidences, they respect those who consistently deliver on their promises.

Part of modern business culture is a focus on the "hard sell" with a drive for immediate profits taking the front seat. You may therefore believe it's right to say anything just to get someone to buy your products, plans, or even be convinced by your ideas.

This tactic involves short-term thinking. As soon as it becomes clear you can't follow through on what you've promised, you'll earn a reputation as unreliable, unprofessional, and possibly even incompetent.

Making sure you deliver on your promises takes careful planning and hard work. You should make sure the projects you're involved in achieve their goals, set clear

## Getting Results without Direct Authority

expectations, and always make an effort to promise less and deliver more.

### Make sure projects achieve their goals

It's essential to work hard to ensure your projects achieve the agreed outcomes. With a track record of success, your level of influence automatically increases. Also, meeting deadlines and quality requirements while staying within a budget demonstrates you're capable of delivering on promises.

### Set expectations

Misunderstandings about what you've promised you'll deliver can result in others feeling you've failed to keep your word.

Establishing the details of what you're promising is the key to setting accurate expectations. Clarify both what you can and can't do, and then ensure you meet the expectations you've set.

### Promise less and deliver more

It's always better to surpass the expectations of others than to promise too much and fail to deliver. Although making unrealistic promises can lure others into supporting you initially, it can only backfire once they realize you make empty promises.

So a general guideline is always to promise less and deliver more. This gives you some leeway if things go wrong and makes it more likely you'll surpass others' expectations.

Take the example of Sara, a representative for a company that makes uniforms. She knows there's a good chance the required garments to a restaurant chain won't be ready for delivery by the date the client originally requested them by.

So she works out a realistic delivery date – and then adds several days to this deadline before consulting with the client. Sara knows that even if unexpected delays occur, she can meet this deadline. And there's a good chance the order can be shipped early to surpass the client's expectations.

Sara sensibly sets realistic expectations and promises less with a view to delivering more. And ultimately, she ensures the order's met successfully and secures a regular client for her company.

By building a reputation as someone able to deliver on her promises, Sara earns herself credibility and greater influence at work.

With her track record of success, Sara has a good reputation with everyone at her company. When she needs to take urgent personal leave, her manager happily obliges, even though company policy dictates a three week notice. Sara's manager trusts her enough to know that an impromptu vacation will not interfere with her long track record of success.

**Question**

In which ways can Sara continue to deliver on her promises and build her credibility?

**Options:**

1. Publish testimonies from satisfied clients

2. Continue giving clients deadlines that give her and her team ample time to complete their work

3. Work to ensure quicker turnaround times to fit in more jobs per month

4. Go through all the details of each job thoroughly with each client, before she provides a price and delivery date

## Answer

Option 1: This option is incorrect. Good advertising might bring in a few more clients, but it won't help Sara deliver on her promises.

Option 2: This option is correct. By promising less, but delivering more, Sara always makes good on her promises.

Option 3: This is incorrect. By getting more clients, Sara may actually decrease the chances she and her team will be able to deliver every job on time.

Option 4: This is a correct option. By carefully determining the details of each job, Sara can give clients realistic quotes and deadlines – ones she and her team will be able to meet.

# ACCEPTING RESPONSIBILITY

### Accepting responsibility
If you always accept responsibility for your actions and give credit where it's due, you'll greatly enhance your credibility. However, if you blame others for your mistakes, accept all the credit for a group effort, or take credit for someone else's work, you'll cause people to distrust you.

So accepting responsibility involves acknowledging the work of others, acknowledging your part in failures, and not blaming others.

### Acknowledging the work of others
By acknowledging the work of others, you appreciate and recognize their contributions. You acknowledge the work fully by being specific when describing contributions and giving credit where credit is due, although without negating your own contribution.

For example, if a coworker helps with a company newsletter by supplying the photographs, you should give her credit. But don't give the impression her contribution outweighs yours or anyone else's.

### Acknowledging your part in failures

When your contributions fail to produce acceptable or desired results, you must be ready to acknowledge your part in the failure. It's best to state what went wrong and your part in this, and then to move forward with suggestions on how to address the failure.

For example, a package you sent isn't delivered because you accidentally transposed the numbers in the address. Admit your mistake and then ensure the package is resent promptly to the correct address.

### Not blaming others

When you do fail, don't blame others – acknowledge your part in the failure. Placing blame for your actions on others is irresponsible and untruthful.

For example, don't blame a coworker who's slightly late in getting you information for your failure to complete a task on time. Instead accept responsibility and don't draw attention to the fact that your coworker's let you down.

Take the example of Arlene, a team leader at a software development company. After a project is completed, her direct superiors call her into a meeting to discuss problems with the software. Arlene's gut response is to lay the blame on errors by some of her team members.

This behavior immediately marks Arlene as lacking in credibility. Even if problems with the software aren't all her fault, her superiors expect her to accept responsibility for the final outcome.

Her team members are also less likely to trust her if they know she blames them for the failures and doesn't credit them for what they do right.

### Question

Which approach do you think Arlene should have taken to boost her credibility?

**Options:**

1. She should have claimed all the faults with the project resulted from insufficient information from the client

2. She should have acknowledged her team's mistakes but accepted the project's failings were ultimately her responsibility

3. She should have presented her superiors with an accurate breakdown of which team members were responsible for which aspects of the project

**Answer**

Option 1: This option is incorrect. Even if the client had provided insufficient information to work with, it would still have been Arlene's responsibility to get the information – even if this meant delaying the project's deadline.

Option 2: This is the correct option. By admitting the buck stops with her, Arlene accepts responsibility for the project's problems. This would enhance her credibility.

Option 3: This option is incorrect. It may be a good idea for Arlene to pinpoint the sources of errors for future projects, but she should have immediately accepted responsibility for not following up and resolving the errors.

If your colleagues don't trust you to take responsibility for your work or to give credit where it's due, you're unlikely to be able to influence them. Conversely, immediately owning up to mistakes and recognizing the work of others will give you credibility – making it more likely others will help you get the results you need.

**Question**

You work on a team in a large events management company.

In which ways can you accept responsibility and therefore gain credibility and influence in the workplace?

**Options:**

1. Ensure you play a role in directing the work of others on your team
2. Show appreciation for every team member's contribution at the end of a project
3. Accurately identify the team members responsible for any errors during team meetings
4. Equally accept any criticism directed at your team even if certain errors weren't entirely your fault

**Answer**

Option 1: This is an incorrect option. You should accept responsibility for your own work and for the part you play in a team's output, rather than attempting to control the work of others – who may even resent your interference.

Option 2: This option is correct. You should acknowledge the work of others and give credit where it's due. This will help motivate colleagues and improve your credibility, as well as your influence.

Option 3: This option is incorrect. Publicly laying the blame for errors on others, even if they did make mistakes, is unlikely to win you credibility – or friends.

Option 4: This is a correct option. By accepting responsibility for the output of your team, you'll build credibility with both team members and managers.

# STRENGTHENING YOUR EXPERTISE

**Strengthening your expertise**

An expert in any field will naturally be considered more credible than someone with less knowledge or fewer skills. Similarly, your credibility and level of influence in the workplace will depend partly on your expertise. Often this will be judged based on your history – have you had successes and shown good judgment in the past? And are you known for providing reliable information?

You can strengthen your expertise in various ways. For example, research your ideas, master the language of your field, cite trusted sources, and team up with credible allies.

**Research your ideas**

The more data you have to support an idea, the more likely it is to be accepted by others. Proper research can also prevent you from making bad calls or providing uninformed opinions, which will reduce your credibility.

**Master the language of your field**

An expert in any field should know that field inside out, and this includes the technical language and terminology that's specific to it. Demonstrating you're a source of expertise doesn't involve just bandying jargon around though – you should fully understand it and be able to use it appropriately.

**Cite trusted sources**

Recognized sources always add weight to a proposal or idea. They may come in different forms, such as articles by respected authorities, endorsements by consultants, or the word of a trusted colleague or superior within your own organization.

**Team up with credible allies**

If you get the support of respected experts, their credibility will give weight to yours. You'll also benefit from their knowledge and notice the glowing reputation of a credible ally will inevitably reflect well on the work you're doing.

Take the example of Oliver, who's a floor manager in a delivery company. He heads a small team of delivery drivers, but is subordinate to several other managers.

Often at company meetings, he'd like to offer what he believes are valuable ideas for increasing profits and efficiency. But he doesn't think his bosses take him seriously.

**Question**

Which actions can Oliver take to strengthen his expertise and thereby build some credibility with his bosses?

**Options:**

1. Quote ideas from reliable trade journals about ways to streamline running costs

2. Keep up to date with industry terminology and all relevant existing jargon

3. Before suggesting any plan of action, read available reports on the topic and speak to team members with on-site experience

4. Ensure his fleet of vehicles is always clean and in good running condition

5. Get other highly regarded managers and drivers to back up his proposals

6. Argue his points with colleagues using scientific evidence from engineering magazines

**Answer**

Option 1: This option is correct. Citing trusted sources is a good way to strengthen his expertise.

Option 2: This option is correct. Mastering the language of his profession demonstrates he knows what he's talking about.

Option 3: This option is correct. Researching the ideas he has is a great way to strengthen his expertise within his field.

Option 4: This option is incorrect. While keeping his fleet in good working order is important, it does nothing to strengthen his expertise.

Option 5: This option is correct. Teaming up with credible allies gives weight to his ideas, and their expertise and credibility boosts his own.

Option 6: This option is incorrect. While doing research is good, trying to disprove others will damage his credibility instead of building it.

# CHAPTER 2 - PERSUASIVE COMMUNICATION

**CHAPTER 2 - Persuasive Communication**
   Section 1 - Using Persuasive Communication to Get Results
   Section 2 - Overcoming Resistance to Get What You Need

# SECTION 1 - USING PERSUASIVE COMMUNICATION TO GET RESULTS

**Section 1 - Using Persuasive Communication to Get Results**

Communicating persuasively is key to getting results when you don't have direct authority over the person you're trying to convince. Proper preparation – knowing what you want and what the other person values – is essential.

Communicating persuasively involves expressing yourself clearly and concisely – getting directly to the point, in simple and confident language. It involves defining the benefits of what you're requesting for the person you're requesting it from, rather than to yourself. And it involves backing up your position with compelling information from credible sources.

# PERSUASIVE COMMUNICATION

**Persuasive communication**
Persuasive communication is key to getting the results you want. Without it, you risk being unclear and therefore misunderstood. In such cases, you won't convince your audience of the value of your words. Imagine reading a request for project funding that's rambling, incoherent, and doesn't explain why the project's a good idea. Would you commit resources to that project?

At one time or another, you've probably found yourself in situations where you need results from someone, but don't have direct authority over them.

For example, you may need to get the cooperation of your team or from someone outside your department to get your own work done.

Or you may want to explain an idea to your boss or get your boss's support on a particular issue.

When you find yourself in situations like these, you need to be convincing. And persuasive communication requires preparation.

Before you approach the person you need help or approval from, you should have a clear idea in your mind about what you want from that person.

Ask yourself – what do I want from this person? What is my goal? If you have a ready answer, you'll be able to get straight to the point when the time comes.

But you also need to consider your request from the other person's perspective.

**The importance of considering other perspectives**

When you understand the perspective of those you're asking for help, you're better able to frame your request in a way that's convincing and appealing.

For example, if a colleague values finding a higher meaning in work beyond just efficiency and personal convenience, she'll probably respond to requests that allow her to feel like she's doing what's "right."

Taking into account the other side's interests will help you be persuasive.

Remember, influence is about trades – you need to offer something the other side values in return for what you want. This means you also need to know what you have to offer that is of value to the other person.

Once you've identified your needs, the interests of the other side, and what you have to offer that aligns with those interests, you'll be ready to ask for what you want. Three strategies can help you be persuasive when you do this: express yourself clearly and directly; define the benefits of what you're requesting; and back up your position with compelling information.

# EXPRESS YOURSELF CLEARLY AND DIRECTLY

**Express yourself clearly and directly**

Nikki's recently started a new job as a graphic designer at an advertising company. She's used to working with newer, more efficient programs than those the advertising company is using. She finds them cumbersome and their output is of poorer quality. It's hindering her work with clients.

Follow along as Nikki talks to her boss, Werner, about upgrading the company's software.

**Werner:** Hi Nikki. I'm glad to see you're settling in. Now what is it you want to discuss with me?

*Werner says, smiling.*

**Nikki:** Well, I'm just wondering about the programs we use for graphic design. The open line work and halftones aren't great. Isn't there something better we could use?

*Nikki complains.*

**Werner:** Oh? I'm not sure exactly what you mean. Do you have something in mind?

*Says Werner, losing interest.*

**Nikki:** You know, there are a lot of good programs out there at the moment.

**Werner:** I'm not sure about changing at this point.

Nikki didn't do a very good job of convincing Werner about the upgrade. She didn't have a clear idea of what she wanted and she used some technical jargon that Werner might not understand. In addition, she ended up asking a vague question that shifted the task of finding a workable solution to Werner, even though he may not even be aware that designers are dissatisfied with the software they're using.

Nikki now takes some time to think about what she wants to say and how to frame the issue in a way that will grab Werner's attention.

Follow along as Nikki once again takes her idea to Werner.

**Werner:** Morning, Nikki.

**Nikki:** Hi Werner. I'd like to talk to you about upgrading the software that's installed on our computers. It has some good features that we can keep, but it's also outdated and inefficient in other ways. I think if we upgrade the software we could offer better results to our clients.

**Werner:** Oh? Go on, I'm listening.

**Question**

What did Nikki do right the second time she approached Werner?

**Options:**

1. She got straight to the point
2. She explained her position in simple, concrete terms
3. She used positive and assertive language

## Getting Results without Direct Authority

4. She set the stage with an introduction

5. She used qualifiers and disclaimers to validate her position

**Answer**

Option 1: This option is correct. Getting straight to the point is important. It helped grab Werner's attention and showed Nikki's confidence in her idea.

Option 2: This is a correct option. Nikki didn't use technical jargon or abstract, ambiguous language. She referred to simple concepts that Werner would understand straight away.

Option 3: This is a correct option. Nikki spoke with confidence in language that would make an impression on Werner. She avoided disclaimers or qualifiers, which might have lessened the impact of her message, or even made Werner skeptical.

Option 4: This option is incorrect. Nikki got straight to the point and told Werner what she wanted. If she had skirted the issue, she might have tried his patience.

Option 5: This is an incorrect option. Nikki used clear and assertive language to get straight to the point, rather than padding her message with disclaimers and qualifiers.

When you approach someone with a request, you should express yourself clearly and directly. What do you want your listener to do, believe in, or think about? Are you asking for support, help, time, or resources? When you explain your position, be concise, direct, and positive and assertive.

**Be concise**

Being concise means you can present your idea, argument, or request clearly in a sentence or two. You can then move on to the details if necessary.

One way to do this is to use language that's simple and unambiguous rather than abstract or filled with unnecessary technical jargon. "The team's made improvements" is better than "the team's implemented several enhancements during the previous quarter."

You should also try to avoid unnecessary intensifiers like "definitely," "really," and "very. These can sound insincere and make others doubt what you're saying.

**Be direct**

It's important to be direct about what you want. It won't help your case if you talk about irrelevant or unrelated issues and take too long to get to the point. Some people may not have a lot of time and if you're asking for more of their time to get the results you want, being direct is particularly important.

You don't want to make people guess what you want. Draw the conclusions for them.

When you're direct, you'll also be more likely to keep their attention and win them over. Long- winded explanations and irrelevant details may put them off helping you.

**Be positive and assertive**

When you're confident, you tend to focus on positive aspects of an issue, downplaying the negative. You use assertive language, which is active and precise, and explains exactly what is happening or going to happen. This type of language engenders trust and cooperation.

Assertive and positive language doesn't rely on disclaimers or qualifiers. For example, "Profits will rise by 25%" sounds more believable than "I think profits may rise by 25%, but I'm not sure."

## Getting Results without Direct Authority

In addition, you should avoid loaded language. This is language that uses words with strong positive or negative connotations that can turn people off. For example, you may get tuned out if you talk about "ways to get clout" to a person who finds the word "clout" negative and somewhat crude.

By expressing yourself clearly and directly, you show you value the other person's time and attention. And this is particularly important when talking to people who have authority over you. They will be more likely to respond positively and have confidence in you.

But while you should be clear and confident, you shouldn't be too abrupt. Remember you're trying to get them on your side, not command that they do something. Expressing yourself clearly and directly is important as you carry out the other strategies – defining the benefits and backing up your position.

# DEFINE THE BENEFITS

**Define the benefits**

Another strategy you can use to communicate persuasively to get the results you want is to describe how others will benefit from helping you. In other words, what's in it for them? Why should they help you, believe you, or support you?

Again, this strategy requires you to prepare beforehand. For example, you should know what their interests are and what motivates them.

Remember, when you don't have direct authority, colleagues you ask for help don't have to agree to assist you. You need to convince them they'll benefit too. But how do you do this? It helps if you reframe your position in terms that appeal to them, think about both gains as well as losses, and ask questions when you need to find out more. It also helps if you tailor your language to fit in with your colleagues' expectations.

**Reframe your position**

The way you frame your position and your choice of language depends on your audiences – their needs, concerns, values, and fears.

For example, if you're persuading your boss that your proposal is good, you might want to frame it in terms of what it can do for the company or how it will improve the reputation of your department.

**Think about both gains and losses**

Benefits come in two different forms – those that give you something you don't have and those that stop you losing something you already have.

For example, you want to convince your manager that your proposal will increase profits. Or you explain that your proposal will prevent losing clients to your competitor.

Highlighting both kinds of benefits illustrates why your proposal is unique. But avoid exaggerating any benefits because obviously hyping them up could offend your audiences.

**Ask questions**

Sometimes you need to ask questions to find out more about your colleagues' interests. You shouldn't ask them how they'll benefit from your idea or from helping you. This is something you need to find out so you can present your request persuasively.

The questions you ask should provide you with good information about what they need. Use questions that encourage reflection. For example, ask "What do you like about the project you're working on?" rather than "Do you like the project?" Your questions should also elicit responses that are clear – for instance, ask "Do you agree?" instead of "OK?"

Another tip is to ask "what" questions before "why" questions, because asking "why" can make others defensive.

**Tailor your language**

In general, you'll be more convincing if you appeal to a person's logic and interests, rather than to some abstract ideal. So instead of saying "This vacuum cleaner has the most powerful motor available" say "This vacuum cleaner is so powerful it can halve the amount of time you spend cleaning your floors."

But you should watch the language you use. If you select words that don't fit in with the culture of your organization or department, you may not have much luck getting the results you're after. For example, if you work in a department where language is expected to be indirect – with requests phrased in terms of organizational benefits rather than personal gains – you shouldn't say something like "If you help me, you'll advance your career." This is too direct.

Now follow along as Nikki tries to persuade Werner that it would be a good idea to upgrade the graphic design software.

**Nikki:** The software we use is outdated. In this industry, that means we don't have the edge over our competitors.

**Werner:** I understand, Nikki, but I'm not sure we have the budget for an upgrade of our software right now.

**Nikki:** The upgrade would pay off in the long run. Newer versions, even of the same program, translate into higher quality designs, faster turnarounds, and we'd be able to keep up with our competition.

### Getting Results without Direct Authority

**Werner:** Yes. I hadn't thought of it that way. But I'm still not sure. Nikki: What do you value in a design, Werner? What would you say our clients

**Werner:** Well, the overriding specification is often that the design is cutting edge. And we pride ourselves on our innovative use of contemporary design trends.

**Nikki:** I agree. And with an upgrade of our software, we'd be able to create better, more up-to-date designs.

Nikki did a good job of listing the benefits for Werner and the company as a whole. She made sure to think in terms of gains and losses – increasing profits and turnarounds, and avoiding losing clients to the competition.

She asked questions to find out what Werner valued, and so was able to reframe her position and tailor her language to appeal to his interests.

If she'd simply said the upgrade would make her job much easier, Werner may not have been as sympathetic to the idea.

# BACK UP YOUR POSITION

**Back up your position**
So far, you've learned how expressing yourself clearly and directly and defining the benefits for the other person can help you persuasively communicate when you don't have direct authority. Another way to be convincing is to back up your position with compelling information. This is especially true if you have an original proposal but are in a position of lower authority. To get approval from management, you need supporting evidence that your idea has value.

Some ways you can provide compelling support for your position is to emphasize your expertise, use credible sources, make numbers memorable, and give examples.

**Emphasize your expertise**
If you have technical experience or expertise in a specific area, say so and provide evidence for it. It shows you know what you're talking about. In turn, your colleague may be more willing to listen to you.

Emphasizing your expertise can be as simple as saying "I came across this problem at the last place I worked and this is how we solved it."

**Use credible sources**

When you quote figures, statistics, testimony, or any other evidence, you should use credible sources to strengthen your argument.

When you use statistics, investigate how the evidence was gathered to check whether it's been skewed in some way or whether another interpretation is possible.

Testimonials can increase your persuasiveness when they come from sources your colleague considers expert and credible. For example, if you want your boss to adopt a new technology, you should provide quotations from respected companies similar to yours that use the technology with great results.

**Make numbers memorable**

People generally switch off when they hear large numbers and complicated statistics – these are too removed from everyday life.

A simple example of how to make a number more memorable is to replace a phrase like "34.5% of employees in this industry" with "more than one in three employees in this room." In this way, you personalize a number and make it more memorable.

**Give examples**

Providing examples can capture the attention of the person you're trying to influence. Examples make generalizations and abstractions more concrete, which helps you make your point.

If you want your boss to give you a raise, you should cite specific examples of work you've done that has contributed to the company's success.

Follow along as Nikki backs up her request for a software upgrade with compelling information.

**Werner:** I'm still not sure the benefits will justify the cost of a complete overhaul of the software system.

**Nikki:** In my experience, the new software is much more efficient. For example, the design I did for the new CallInsure logo took me four days to complete at the office. But a similar design I did at home using the newer program took me only two days. If you like, I can download the trial version and show you what I mean.

**Werner:** That is a big difference.

**Nikki:** I've asked around – two out of three designers who work here say they'd find it easier to do their work on the new software I'm proposing we use.

**Werner:** Wow. I didn't realize the situation was that bad.

**Nikki:** Not to mention our closest competitors all endorse this software. Take a look at this article.

**Werner:** Nikki, you've convinced me. I'll make a recommendation to the Finance Department. Thanks for bringing this to my attention.

**Nikki:** No problem! Thanks for hearing me out.

Nikki stressed her technical experience and backed up her request with compelling information. She made the information more memorable by showing what a difference new software could make to a single project.

She made numbers memorable and relevant, and cited credible sources, such as the other designers and the company's competitors, to back up her argument.

## Getting Results without Direct Authority

**Question**

What are effective ways to communicate persuasively to get the results you need?

**Options:**

1. Avoid intensifying words like "extremely"
2. Be brief, but avoid being abrupt or commanding
3. Use data to justify your position, but make it interesting and memorable
4. Use technical jargon to prove you know what you're talking about
5. Explain how your idea or suggestion will make your job easier for you
6. Reframe your position in a way that's appealing to the person you need help from
7. Explain what the other person will get out of it

**Answer**

Option 1: This option is correct. Intensifying words only detract from the core of your message and might make your listener skeptical. Instead, use simple phrases to say exactly what you mean.

Option 2: This is a correct option. While you should get to the point and be as concise as possible, you should avoid being too abrupt, which could seem rude or demanding.

Option 3: This option is correct. To justify your position, you should back it up with evidence that's compelling.

Option 4: This option is incorrect. While you should stress your technical expertise where relevant, you should use simple, commonly used words to make your point concisely and forcefully.

Option 5: This is an incorrect option. You should frame the benefits of your idea in a way that will interest others – for example, in terms of productivity or profitability, if that's what they value most or are interested in.

Option 6: This option is correct. When you present your request for help, you need to consider how helping will benefit the other person. In this way, you'll be more persuasive.

Option 7: This is a correct option. You should spell out what the other person will gain from fulfilling your request, rather than explaining how you'll benefit yourself.

**Question**

What are the benefits of being able to communicate persuasively?

**Options:**

1. You'll be able to get the results you need
2. Others will have more confidence in you
3. You'll be able to make people do what you want for your personal benefit
4. Others will understand the importance of your own values and concerns

**Answer**

Option 1: This is a correct option. Communicating persuasively is key to getting the results you need from people, especially when you don't have the direct authority to make them fulfill your requests. When you're able to fully explain the benefits to them, you'll find they respond more positively to your requests or proposals.

Option 2: This option is correct. Because you're clear, use credible sources, and demonstrate you take others' interests into account, people will have more confidence in your ideas, opinions, or suggestions.

Option 3: This is an incorrect option. Persuasive communication involves showing people how your suggestions or ideas will benefit them, not you.

Option 4: This option is incorrect. While you'll be able to show others how your ideas or requests are beneficial to them, you can only do this by appealing to their interests and concerns, rather than changing them.

# SECTION 2 - OVERCOMING RESISTANCE TO GET WHAT YOU NEED

**Section 2 - Overcoming Resistance to Get What You Need**

No matter how much you've prepared in advance, you can still come across resistance when you're trying to get help in situations where you don't have direct authority. You can overcome resistance by adapting your approach, showing understanding of the resister's emotions, listening to the resister's concerns, and giving a two-sided argument.

If you're able to overcome resistance, you become more persuasive and are more likely to achieve what you want.

# OVERCOMING RESISTANCE

**Overcoming resistance**

At some point in your career, you're likely to encounter colleagues who, for one reason or another, resist your request for help. And this resistance may put your plans to achieve a specific result in jeopardy.

The reason for resistance may lie in the fact that your colleagues, whose help you request, are committed to other projects or disagree with your plans on technical grounds.

To overcome resistance, you may use different strategies:
- adapting your approach,
- showing an understanding of the emotions of the resister,
- listening to the concerns of the resister, and
- giving a two-sided argument.

# ADAPTING YOUR APPROACH

**Adapting your approach**

To overcome resistance, you may need to adapt your approach. You should resist the temptation to keep pressing. Instead, work out the resistor's values and then change your approach appropriately.

Instead of pressing and trying to persuade, it's far more useful for you to find out how the resister would like to be approached. How can you make your idea more appealing? It helps to find out more about what values are important to the resister, and use those to adapt your approach.

Consider Todd, whose company's marketing strategy is based solely on promoting the quality of its products. Todd wants to propose a new marketing idea in which a certain percentage of sales are donated to selected charities. The production manager, Jessica, doesn't agree and Todd has to figure out a way of overcoming her resistance.

Follow along as Todd tries to convince Jessica about his idea.

## Getting Results without Direct Authority

**Todd:** Jessica, I think you'll like the idea if you let me explain it to you in more detail.

**Jessica:** Well, I'm not sure.

**Todd:** It's an innovative marketing strategy whose benefits have been documented in various trade magazines.

**Jessica:** I really have no time to wade through those magazines, Todd. I'm sorry.

**Todd:** I know how busy you are so I thought I could collate the important points into a short report. Then you can read it when you have some time.

**Jessica:** Well...

**Todd:** I'll stick to the facts.

**Jessica:** I suppose I could take some time out to read a brief report. As long as you keep it to facts only!

**Todd:** Of course, facts only. I'll make it brief and to the point. And please note there's no hurry. This is a long term strategy after all.

**Jessica:** Right, I will.

**Todd:** Thank you again for your time Jessica. I do appreciate it.

In this conversation, Todd begins to push Jessica to listen to his idea. But Jessica doesn't like this approach so Todd focuses instead on what he's learned about Jessica's values – in particular, how she places great value on time and people getting to the point. In this way, he becomes more persuasive and may get her to support his idea.

# UNDERSTANDING EMOTIONS

**Understanding emotions**

In addition to adapting your approach, showing an understanding of someone's emotions can help you overcome resistance. These emotions may not be immediately apparent, so you may need to ask questions to find out more about how the other person's feeling.

Once you have an idea of the emotions, you can address them.

Many different emotions can arise when you present colleagues with new ideas or when you ask them for help on something. They may feel excited and enthusiastic. However, other emotions can encourage a colleague to resist you. Most people's resistance stems from feelings of distrust or fear.

**Distrust**

Distrust stems from the relationship you have with your colleagues. If they distrust you, they're resisting you, rather than your idea.

To be persuasive, you need to have good relationships with those you want to persuade because then they'll be more inclined to trust you. You may need to work on your relationship with your colleagues before you can convince them to help you.

**Fear**

If resisters are fearful, they're worried about something – maybe they fear the idea won't work or that if they help you it will affect their own work negatively.

It helps to address any fears you think resisters may have. You may need to clarify their concerns or fears first by listening carefully to them and asking questions. When you do this, you can address the fears directly, showing that you understand them and are capable of sorting out key issues of concern.

In Todd's case, if Jessica is resisting his marketing idea because she has a problem with him rather than the idea, the relationship between them has to improve.

If, for example, Jessica finds Todd unrealistic or speculative, he may need to demonstrate his seriousness by paying attention to detail when preparing for his pitch and by using quantitative data and qualitative evidence that she finds reassuring.

Or Jessica is resisting because of fear. In this case, Todd should listen to Jessica's concerns and address them directly. For example, he might reassure her by saying the implementation won't take a great deal of time, but also point out it will require some research into an appropriate charity, which he's willing to do.

# LISTENING TO CONCERNS

**Listening to concerns**

It's very important that you listen to the concerns of those who resist helping you. This builds trust in your relationship with them. Listening is key in demonstrating to others that you understand them and value their input. By showing the resisters you take their thoughts and concerns seriously, they will be more inclined to listen to your idea.

You can use two strategies to show you're listening:
- paraphrasing, and
- clarifying the issues resisters may have.

**Paraphrasing**

Rewording and reflecting back what someone has said is an effective way of showing you're listening and care about what the resister is saying.

Paraphrasing gets the resister to respond to you. For example, you can reword a concern into a question: "So you say that if you help with this project you won't be able to finish your own?" It's likely the resister agrees with you, which helps to establish common ground and make the individual more receptive to your idea or request.

**Clarifying issues**

When the resister is giving you feedback, you should identify the main concerns and summarize them.

For example, Todd might say to Jessica "So you have two main concerns. The first one is probably the most important, right?" In this way, you establish a level of understanding and agreement that can help you overcome resistance. You also indicate you're able to identify the key issues.

# GIVING A TWO-SIDED ARGUMENT

**Giving a two-sided argument**
Another strategy you may use when you're faced with someone who resists your request or idea is to give a two-sided argument. This requires you to acknowledge the resister's arguments first and then follow it up with your counter-arguments. When you use this approach, the resister may be more open to discussion and may participate in solving the problem at hand.

When you present your argument, you need to clearly address the resister's concerns and provide powerful answers that make opposition less likely. When possible, you should also demonstrate how you've incorporated the resister's ideas, interests, values, and concerns into your solution.

This requires a certain amount of preparation or you won't be able to anticipate all arguments based on the resister's interests and values.

Consider how Todd prepares a two-sided argument. He brainstorms possible objections to his idea by examining time, materials, expense, and risk. Then he

## Getting Results without Direct Authority

develops his counter-arguments, drawing on the likely objections.

Follow along as Todd presents a two-sided argument to Jessica.

**Todd:** Jessica, thanks for reading the report I sent you and agreeing to meet with me to discuss my proposal for a new marketing strategy.

**Todd:** Before we discuss the proposal in more detail, I want to address some issues you might be concerned about. First, with regard to expense, I did some research and calculations and found that our initial outlay is within reason and we can recoup it within the first couple of months. I've written up a short report to back this up.

**Jessica:** Well, that's good because I was wondering about that. This report clearly supports what you say with good evidence. That's something I can work with.

**Todd:** And we won't need to hire new employees to implement the strategy. I know the company isn't keen on taking on anyone new right now.

**Jessica:** That's correct. But how many work hours will we have to spend setting this up?

**Todd:** If two employees spent just two hours once a week on implementing the new strategy, we'll have it set up in three weeks. Two hours a week shouldn't have too much of an impact on production and I think the results will be worth it.

**Jessica:** You've certainly put a lot of thought into this strategy and have touched on all my concerns.

Todd presents a two-sided argument. His research and statistics take Jessica by surprise, but she's willing to listen to him. Todd increases Jessica's confidence in him because he demonstrates an understanding of the key issues and presents them convincingly.

**Question**

Suppose you need help from a colleague but he shows resistance. Your relationship with him hasn't been great in the past and he seems to distrust your motives.

How can you effectively overcome his resistance?

**Options:**

1. Find out more about what he values and change your approach so it incorporates these values

2. Focus on building trust and improving your relationship with your colleague

3. Paraphrase your colleague's concerns

4. Determine what your colleague's arguments might be and prepare to address these first

5. Persist in getting your colleague's help by sending e-mails and setting up meetings to keep him focused on its importance

6. Focus on how his helping you will benefit you and show him how it could harm your career if he doesn't

**Answer**

Option 1: This is a correct option. Adapting your approach based on what your colleague is interested in can help you overcome his resistance.

Option 2: This option is correct. If you don't have a good relationship with the colleague you need help from, resistance can be greater. To overcome resistance based on negative emotions such as distrust, you may need to work on your relationship with your colleague first.

Option 3: This is a correct option. Showing you're listening to and understanding your colleague's concerns encourages him to listen to your arguments. By

## Getting Results without Direct Authority

paraphrasing a concern, you tell him you've heard, understood, and are taking it into account.

Option 4: This option is correct. By preparing in advance for possible arguments, you can counteract them effectively and be more persuasive.

Option 5: This is an incorrect option. You should resist the temptation to keep pressing your colleague. This could increase his resistance.

Option 6: This option is incorrect. It's important to focus on your colleague's views rather than your own. You need to understand why he's resisting. You may need to adapt your approach and show you understand his concerns.

# CHAPTER 3 - RECIPROCITY

**CHAPTER 3 - Reciprocity**
 Section 1 - Developing a Give-and-Take Strategy to Get Results
 Section 2 - Identifying Trades for Those You Want to Influence
 Section 3 - Determining Your Trading Approach to Get Results

# SECTION 1 - DEVELOPING A GIVE-AND-TAKE STRATEGY TO GET RESULTS

**Section 1 - Developing a Give-and-Take Strategy to Get Results**

To influence people to do something for you, you need to do something for them or give them something they value.

To develop an effective give-and-take strategy, you take four steps – determine exactly what your needs are, consider your relationship with the other person, determine the needs of the other person, and identify the resources you have on offer.

# THE GIVE-AND-TAKE STRATEGY

**The give-and-take strategy**

The Scottish proverb "Give and take makes good friends" alludes to the concept of reciprocity: good relationships are formed and maintained when each party is willing to give and take. In other words, if you help me with something, I'll help you in return.

Reciprocity is a universal concept and applies to all kinds of interactions – not just friendship. If you want to influence your colleagues to do something, you need to do something for them or give them something they value.

In short, exchange is the foundation of influence.

For example, if you want your boss to give you more responsibility, you should show how this will benefit him – what your boss will get in exchange.

A benefit of being able to use a reciprocal give-and-take strategy is that it can help you achieve your goals.

This is because you're better able to get the support or approval from those you depend on.

And a give-and-take strategy helps you to get more done because you're able to make use of others and their resources — adding strength to your work.

But for such an exchange to work, you must be positive about the people you need help from. If you start off assuming they won't want to help you, you deprive yourself of an accurate understanding of them — which can harm your chances of securing their cooperation or even turn them into adversaries. Thus it's vital to positively assume that everyone is a potential ally.

And you need to understand the concerns, objectives, and styles of those you want to influence in order to know what to offer in exchange for their help.

This is particularly true when you don't know those you want to approach for help. By knowing what drives people, you're more likely to find an effective way to influence them.

However, it's also important to know what you want and what resources you have access to — because you can only offer something that you already have or have access to.

To develop an effective give-and-take strategy to influence others, then, you should determine your needs, consider your relationship with the other person, determine the other person's needs, and identify the resources you can offer.

# DETERMINING YOUR OWN NEEDS

**Determining your own needs**

Before you elicit help from someone, you should know what you need. Only then will you be able to clearly communicate your needs to others.

**Most important considerations**

Important considerations are your primary goals, the timespan of these goals, the necessity of the goals, and whether the goals are more important than your relationship with the person or group.

You should ask yourself several questions when you consider your needs:

- What are my primary goals in seeking this person's cooperation?
- Are my goals short-term or long-term?
- Are my goals "needs" or just "nice-to-haves"?
- Is my priority to accomplish a goal or is it to preserve or improve my relationship with this person?

It's important to separate your personal desires from what you actually need. You do this so that you don't

## Getting Results without Direct Authority

forget your task goals or prevent yourself from listening to the needs of others.

You don't need to deny all your personal desires – but just make sure you're clear on your priorities.

But even when you're clear on your primary goals, it's important to be flexible in how you achieve those goals. Flexibility may lead you to solutions that are better than what you first envisioned.

As a rule, you should hold on to the essence of your goal, but be open to alterations as you work with others whose cooperation you need. Glen is a journalist at a newspaper. He's enthusiastic and eager to advance quickly.

Glen currently works across different departments, but his speciality is sports – especially extreme sports. The newspaper doesn't cover these kinds of sports, so Glen would love to introduce this stream of work into the Sports Department.

Glen also likes being in charge, and he's got his sights on eventually heading the Sports Department. However, that goal seems a long way off because most of his recent assignments have been centered around politics.

For Glen to move into the Sports Department permanently, he needs the help of Andrew, the sports editor. All Andrew needs to do is ask the newspaper's managing editor to transfer Glen.

Andrew can also be an essential ally if he supports Glen's wish to contribute extreme sports articles to the newspaper and to move up the ladder in the Sports Department.

Andrew, a seasoned sports journalist, enjoys his role as sports editor and occasional writer. However, he dislikes the administrative work that comes with managing a writing team. He fears that assigning a new journalist to the department will add to his administrative burden, so he's reluctant to bring in Glen.

**Question**

Glen believes Andrew can be a real help to him, but he first needs to clearly define what he needs from Andrew.

How should Glen determine his own needs?

**Options:**

1. Write down how he will achieve his primary goal but be open to change
2. Determine what resources he can offer as a trade
3. Decide which of his goals is most important
4. Separate his goals from his personal aspiration
5. Identify the best strategy to get Andrew's help

**Answer**

To effectively determine your needs, you must prioritize your goals, be flexible, and separate your personal desires from your goals.

Option 1: This is a correct option. Glen thinks that the only way to get into the Sports Department is for Andrew to make a special request to the managing editor. But Andrew may choose a different approach, so Glen needs to be flexible enough to accept that another approach might also work.

Option 2: This option is incorrect. Glen only needs to consider his potential trade items later in the process. At this point, he needs to focus on clearly defining his own needs.

Option 3: This is a correct option. Although Andrew can help Glen to achieve a number of goals, Glen must

## Getting Results without Direct Authority

focus on the most important of these goals – getting into the Sports Department.

Option 4: This option is correct. Glen aspires to head the sports department, but for now he must focus on achieving his more immediate goals.

Option 5: This is an incorrect option. Although Glen needs this strategy, at this point he should focus on clearly defining his own needs.

# CONSIDERING YOUR RELATIONSHIP

**Considering your relationship**

When you need others to help you get the results you want, it's important to consider your relationships with them. If you have a good relationship with your colleague, for example, it's usually easier to make your request. However, if you're on bad terms, you may need to ease into the request. For particularly strained relationships, it's better to first resolve the tension that exists between your colleague and you.

To assess your relationship with your colleagues ask yourself: How well do I know my colleagues? What is my perception of them? How might I approach them? Awareness of your current relationship with your colleagues can help you choose the right way to address them. For example, if you perceive that someone is irrational, you may be responding to him with this perception in mind. Recognizing this can open you to developing a more positive way of approaching him.

To initiate or improve a relationship with your colleagues whose help you want, you may need to think about altering your work style to align with theirs. It's also important to consider their background and personality.

**Work style**

Different people work in different ways. Some favor creativity and lack of structure, while others are statistically-minded, preferring detailed analysis of a situation.

You need to know their preferred style, as well as your own, so you can approach them in a way that's most appealing to their taste.

And remember – if you aren't aware of your style, it can keep you from considering other possible approaches and hinder your ability to connect.

**Background and personality**

Each person has unique history, values, preferences, and goals. Something urgent, exciting, or extremely important to you may mean nothing to another person.

Consider how your personality and background relates to your colleagues. What are the differences? This will help you better understand your current relationship and how you might develop a future relationship with them.

Remember Glen, the journalist? Glen needs to consider his relationship with Andrew – the person he's seeking to forge an alliance with.

Unfortunately, the two hardly have a relationship – they've exchanged pleasantries once, maybe twice. And when Glen thinks about it, he realizes he's intimidated by Andrew's reputation and stature at the newspaper.

Glen knows his own work style is chaotic and unstructured. This is very different from Andrew, who works in a methodical, tightly-managed style.

Glen has also observed that Andrew enjoys researching stories and he's usually in a good mood when discussing his favorite basketball team, who are the reigning champions of the national league.

**Question**

Which factors has Glen considered about his current relationship with Andrew?

**Options:**

1. How he can adapt his own work style to Andrew's work style
2. His perception of Andrew as a daunting figure
3. Andrew's attitude toward authority at the magazine
4. How persuasive Glen can be when asking Andrew for help
5. How well he knows Andrew

**Answer**

Option 1: This option is correct. Glen may be more successful if he takes a more structured, methodical approach – which Andrew favors.

Option 2: This is a correct option. Recognizing his fear of Andrew's reputation may help Glen work to develop a relationship that goes beyond intimidation.

Option 3: This option is incorrect. Andrew's attitude toward authority has no bearing on Glen and Andrew's relationship.

Option 4: This is an incorrect option. Glen's persuasiveness will be important when he approaches Andrew, but it's not a factor in their current relationship.

Option 5: This option is correct. Considering they have only a formal relationship helps Glen to determine how he should approach Andrew.

# DETERMINING THE OTHER PERSON'S NEEDS

**Determining the other person's needs**

In addition to knowing your own needs, you must consider several aspects of your colleagues' needs:
- your colleagues' tasks and responsibilities – including deadlines – which will impact their willingness to help you,
- who your colleagues interact with at work – because everyone they deal with will create pressures that affect the way they look at problems and requests,
- how your colleagues' performance is measured and rewarded – because they're more likely to help you if it boosts their own work, and
- your colleagues' career aspirations – because if you can offer something that advances their career, they're more likely to help you.

To find this information, you can use a number of methods, including doing research, asking your colleagues directly, and observing behavior.

When "asking" and "observing behavior," it's important to be aware of clues that your colleagues may reveal. These clues may show you what's important to them.

Clues may come from body language, choice of words, tone, and the types of concerns raised.

**Body language**

Sometimes body language can communicate more than what words express. For example, it may reveal a person's enthusiasm, attentiveness, or annoyance.

It's useful to pay attention to body language so that you can respond appropriately to it. Watch for facial expressions, physical gestures, and posture that may indicate a negative attitude, for example.

**Choice of words**

The language people use can reveal a lot about what's important to them.

For example, managers who come from sporting backgrounds may use sports-related phrases when they speak.

Or business analysts whose bonus is heavily dependent on key performance indicators may pepper their sentences with the term "KPI."

**Tone**

You can pick up a lot about people's thoughts by the tone of voice, volume, and the rate at which they speak.

For example, if a particular work task doesn't inspire someone, you may well hear the disinterest in this person's voice. Or, if the person is discussing an issue he feels sensitive about, he might lower the volume so that others don't hear.

**Types of concerns raised**

People will often voice their concerns directly, saying things like "I'm worried about the costs" or "The marketing people won't agree to that."

You might read these statements as signs of stubbornness, but they can also be viewed as indicators of what's important to someone.

Asking questions, rather than arguing, can open further dialog.

Taking a direct approach and asking people about their interests, values, and concerns can offer benefits. People may reveal a lot more than you expect. They want to explain themselves and their situation. Moreover, sincerity and directness in your inquiry creates openness and trust in the relationship.

**Question**

Glen needs to determine Andrew's needs. But, he doesn't know much about Andrew.

Which are the best methods Glen can use to find out about Andrew's needs?

**Options:**

1. Ask the managing editor if Andrew has taken any stress-related leave in the past

2. Ask Andrew for advice on how to work effectively with him

3. Do some research into Andrew's professional background and recent work

4. Observe Andrew's choice of words and the issues he tends to raise regarding work

5. Explain his needs to Andrew first, so Andrew knows what he requires

**Answer**

Three ways to determine the other person's needs are research, asking directly, and observing their behavior.

Option 1: This is an incorrect option. It's inappropriate to ask Andrew's superior about such a personal issue.

Option 2: This option is correct. This direct question can give Glen clues as to how Andrew likes to work and what's important to him.

Option 3: This is a correct option. This research can give Glen clues about Andrew's areas of interest and career ambitions.

Option 4: This option is correct. Observing Andrew's language and the issues he raises gives Glen clues to what's important to Andrew.

Option 5: This option is incorrect. At this point, the focus needs to be on finding out about Andrew.

Glen makes an effort to learn about Andrew's professional history and interests, his career aspirations, and how he is rewarded.

**Professional history and interests**

After a few years as a journalist, Andrew took a break to study psychology – a field which he thoroughly enjoys.

**Career aspirations**

One of Andrew's biggest aspirations is to write a book about how his favorite basketball team's recent championship win united the local community, which was previously divided along racial lines. He recently started work on the book.

**How he is rewarded**

Andrew's team often produces superb, award-winning pieces of sports journalism. Andrew is proud that he's often invited to speak at local and national media association events, and accepts the awards on his team's behalf.

By determining the other person's needs, as well as your own, you'll ensure you make a fair trade – one that benefits both you and the person you need help from. And by showing interest in the other person's needs and responding to those needs, you actively build better relationships.

# IDENTIFYING YOUR RESOURCES

**Identifying your resources**

To make that fair trade with people you need help from, you should identify the resources that may be valuable to them.

You want to find something that is acceptable and valuable enough to motivate them to give you what you need.

What resources could you offer? It all depends on what you find out about the other person. And, the resource has to be something you possess or have direct access to.

People tend to value different things. For example, someone might value being involved in a task that has larger significance for society, while another may want to obtain more personnel for a project. Someone else may value being recognized for an accomplishment.

Glen hopes to secure Andrew's help in getting a transfer to the Sports Department. However, to be persuasive, Glen may need to offer Andrew something in return.

Glen recalls that Andrew's interested in psychology, enjoys receiving awards on behalf of his team, and hopes

## Getting Results without Direct Authority

to publish a book about how his basketball's championship-winning season united the local community.

Glen thinks Andrew will appreciate these resources:
- using the managing editor's sports psychology book,
- introducing Andrew to Glen's basketball player friends, or
- doing research for one of Andrew's upcoming stories.

**Question**

Which resource should Glen offer as a trade in this situation?

**Options:**

1. Using the managing editor's sports psychology book to add a new dimension to Andrew's stories

2. Introducing Andrew to Glen's basketball player friends, who play for Andrew's favorite team and who Andrew can interview for his book

3. Doing research for one of Andrew's upcoming stories to save Andrew the trouble of research

**Answer**

You shouldn't offer resources that don't hold value to the other person. You also shouldn't offer resources that don't belong to you or resources that you don't have direct access to. You should only offer resources you possess or have direct access to, ensuring that the resources are valuable to the other person.

Option 1: This option is incorrect. Glen should not offer a resource that does not belong to him.

Option 2: This is the correct option. This offer is very valuable and attractive to Andrew because it can help him in his career ambition of writing a book about how the basketball team's championship win united the local community.

Option 3: This is an incorrect option. Andrew enjoys doing his own research, so this offer isn't really valuable to him.

**Question**

What are the benefits of being able to use a give-and-take strategy?

**Options:**

1. Helps you to carry out fair trades
2. Helps you to build positive, long-term relationships
3. Keeps the focus on what you need
4. Helps you achieve your goals
5. Gives you more authority over your colleagues

**Answer**

Option 1: This is a correct option. Using a give-and-take strategy enables you to meet your own needs as well as the other person's needs.

Option 2: This option is correct. One of the steps in developing a give-and-take strategy is to learn about the other person's needs, environment, and work style. This can help you understand the other person and build a better relationships.

Option 3: This is an incorrect option. One of the steps in developing a give-and-take strategy is finding out what you need, but you must also find out about the other person to be reciprocal.

Option 4: This option is correct. Using a give-and-take strategy adds strength to your work by drawing on the expertise and resources of other people.

## Getting Results without Direct Authority

Option 5: This is an incorrect option. Using a give-and-take strategy does not necessarily give you more authority. The strategy merely enables you to achieve results without formal authority.

# SECTION 2 - IDENTIFYING TRADES FOR THOSE YOU WANT TO INFLUENCE

**Section 2 - Identifying Trades for Those You Want to Influence**

The give and take of reciprocal relationships is a part of everyday life, including that in organizations.

You can identify trade objects for reciprocity by the type of reward they offer the recipient. Task-related trade objects relate to something immediate that will help recipients get their jobs done. Career-related trade objects help the recipients enhance their careers. Relationship-related trade objects help recipients strengthen useful or beneficial relationships, and inspiration-related trade objects help provide meaning for the work the recipients do.

# TYPES OF RECIPROCAL TRADE OBJECTS

**Types of reciprocal trade objects**

How many times have you heard the expression "You scratch my back and I'll scratch yours?" Reciprocal exchanges – trading something of value in return for what you want or need – happen all the time in organizations. For example, you do the work you're assigned and you get pay and benefits, or you support a colleague's project and he then offers to help you with a report you're working on.

Common trade objects in business relate to people's ability to do their jobs – for example obtaining assistance on a project or getting access to certain information. But there are other types of trade objects too – think of a sales manager who ignores his secretary leaving early on some days in return for her staying late to finish compiling an urgent report. In this topic, you'll learn about several common types of trade objects – trades related to tasks, career, relationships, and inspiration.

# TASK-RELATED TRADES

**Task-related trades**

Task-related trade objects, as the name implies, are ones that help you get a job done. For example, if you need information from a colleague – what better way to get your colleague's help than by offering to assist with a tough assignment she's working on?

You're probably able to recall many task-related trade objects, but these are the most common ones:
- assistance with existing tasks or projects,
- information that can help with a job,
- more challenge to improve skills,
- new resources to assist with a task or project,
- organizational support for a job, and
- rapid response to help speed up a job.

**Assistance**

Most people have tasks or jobs they'd like to be rid of or at least receive help with. When people are faced with a job they dislike, they can't cope with, or don't have enough time for, assistance can be a valuable trade object.

If you want to gain influence with someone who seems to be in this situation, you might offer help.

Assistance can also mean providing products or services to another department. To make this trade valuable, the department providing the services or products may need to learn about and adjust to the receiving department's needs.

**Information**

Everyone knows that knowledge is power. Many people value knowledge that helps them excel – from specific answers to questions about industry trends, customer issues, what other departments are doing, and the strategic views of management. Do you know someone who values this kind of information? If you have access to such knowledge, you may be able to use it as a trade object.

To increase your opportunities of using this type of trade, you may want to cultivate wide-ranging relationships throughout your organization, staying informed about what's going on around you and gaining as much experience in aspects of the organization as possible.

**More challenge**

In modern business, challenge is highly valued because it helps improve skills and gives people the opportunity to prove themselves. How can you challenge someone? Get the person to help solve a problem or perform difficult tasks that the individual usually doesn't encounter.

And if you have a boss who likes a challenge, you might consider sharing difficult work-related problems with him. Or you might point to difficult issues that your boss can address with his own superiors.

## New resources

Trade objects related to new resources depend on the work context. If resources are in short supply, or an employee or manager desperately needs something specific to reach a goal, then a new resource is extremely valuable. These can take the form of an increased budget, additional employees, new equipment, or even new office space.

For example, an administrator allocates much-needed scientific equipment to the Research Department in return for getting a key project prioritized.

## Organizational support

Who values organizational support? Someone who's working on a project and needs support in selling the project to others might support this trade object. If someone is trying to push a proposal or trying complete a difficult project, an endorsement from a superior or a trusted colleague can give him a much-needed boost.

Imagine a copy writer who proposes a bold idea for a campaign. Her idea gets a hostile reception from many of her colleagues, but a well-placed word from the department head could change minds and be used as currency for a future favor.

## Rapid response

A rapid response to a request, message, or enquiry can be valuable, especially if these are urgent. Helping colleagues jump ahead on a waiting list or get what they want quickly is excellent currency to have if you want to gain influence with them.

For example, you're in a position of allocating company resources and you make special effort to ensure a certain manager gets what he needs to complete a project early.

He, in turn, offers you assistance with a report you're compiling.

# CAREER-RELATED TRADES

**Career-related trades**

Career-related trade objects are another form of practical exchange, although they may not necessarily appeal to the other person's immediate needs. These objects are intended to improve the other person's career, either by making that person look good or by offering something tangible toward that end.

For example, if you help someone with a high profile project, you may increase your recognition and reputation in the company. What are other career-related trade objects? Besides improved reputation and increased recognition, career-related trade objects include a chance to feel important, the opportunity to make contacts, and the chance to be on the "inside."

**Improved reputation**

A good reputation is the result of positive recognition built over time. It is immensely valuable as a trade object. Why? A person who has a good reputation gets invited to important meetings, is approached about new projects, and is consulted about decisions.

Just as a good reputation can open doors, a bad reputation can limit a person's potential growth. If you want to get help from others to get the results you need at work, it's important to act in a way that enhances your reputation. If you exhibit negative behavior or attitude, you may get a reputation that hinders you from getting the help you need.

**Increased recognition**

Recognition can be a powerful motivator for people to do extra work or go above and beyond the call of duty. In particular, if you manage employees, it always pays to spread credit around.

For example, you might influence someone to help you on a project if you state that a key manager is interested in the result and will take notice of everyone who's involved.

**Chance to feel important**

The chance to feel important can be valuable currency for trade, especially for a person who feels undervalued or unnoticed.

For example, a secretary whose work goes largely unnoticed despite her efforts to keep her department running smoothly may find this a valuable trade object. A heartfelt thank you and the mention of her contribution at a monthly meeting gives her motivation to continue doing excellent work.

**Opportunity to make contacts**

The opportunity to make contacts is valuable because it helps you create a network of people who can be approached when needed for mutually helpful interactions.

Take the example of a lawyer who's moved to a city she doesn't know. If you can provide her with introductions to useful people, you'll earn yourself gratitude and a favor in return.

**Chance to be on the "inside"**

Being part of the inner circle can be a valuable trade object because it provides its members access to information and contacts. They're also often included in making important decisions, planning, and events, which boosts recognition.

Take the example of inviting an office manager to sit in on committee meetings when decisions regarding future company plans are made. Such inclusion offers this manager many opportunities and constitutes valuable currency.

# RELATIONSHIP-RELATED TRADES

**Relationship-related trades**
Relationship-related trade objects have more to do with strengthening a relationship with someone than directly accomplishing tasks. Acceptance, understanding, and personal support are among the relationship-related trade objects you may consider using.
**Acceptance**
Some individuals value acceptance or a sense of inclusion – a feeling that they're close to others. They like personal warmth and friendly behavior. And though this doesn't mean they place this type of closeness over task-related trade objects, they won't find it easy to deal with people who're not warm and accepting.
**Understanding**
A demonstration of understanding and sympathy can be highly valued by anyone who feels stressed, isolated, or lacking support. Being able to provide an impartial ear for someone in need is a rare skill and can be used as a currency.

Do you know someone who feels particularly overwhelmed by a tough task? Perhaps he gets a lot of practical advice or hears about his colleagues' problems in response. If you give him relief in the form of listening and sympathy, he's likely to feel grateful.

Being listened to can be a valuable trade object.

**Personal support**

For some individuals, having the support of others is very valuable, particularly at difficult times.

If a colleague in your department, for example, is feeling stressed, or vulnerable, he's likely to appreciate and remember a kind gesture, such as asking how he's doing, or making a thoughtful comment.

Just be careful you don't cross any boundaries in making your gesture.

# INSPIRATION-RELATED TRADES

**Inspiration-related trades**

How many people can say their job helps change the world for the better? Very few, if you ask them, which is why inspiration-related trade objects have value for people. Given the option to work for a paycheck or work for a paycheck and improve living conditions in East Africa, which would you choose?

Inspiration-related trade objects focus on inspirational goals that offer meaning to the work someone does. For example, you might offer a colleague the chance to achieve a greater vision, do something well, or do the right thing.

**Achieve a greater vision**

Most people wouldn't pass up the opportunity to be part of something big. If you're able to paint an exciting vision of your company or department's future, you can inspire others to help you achieve it. An inspiring vision can help overcome objections and inconvenience by those you need help from.

Take the example of a team of architects working on the plans for an upmarket hotel. With a deadline fast approaching, their manager motivates them to put in extra hours by making them proud of being part of this grand building's creation.

**Do something well**

Many people want to excel at their job, so giving someone the opportunity to demonstrate quality craftsmanship or skills is highly motivating. Offering your colleagues a chance to perform quality work can be a valuable trade object when you need to get their cooperation to achieve your results.

Suppose you need the help of an editor to finish a manuscript. To get that help, you tell her that working on the manuscript allows her to demonstrate the high quality of her work in an influential publication.

**Do the right thing**

A lot of people want to live their lives according to moral or ethical standards but may feel this isn't possible in their job. If you can provide others with an opportunity to perform a task that gives them the feeling they're doing the right thing, you may find they're willing to help you. This is particularly true for those who value a higher standard than just getting work done efficiently.

For example, you approach an accountant to help on a project for a charity organization. While the pay is below what he receives in the corporate sector, and the hours are inconvenient, the chance to do something good motivates him to help you achieve the results you need.

**Question**

Match the examples to the appropriate categories of trade objects you can offer to gain influence.

### Getting Results without Direct Authority

**Options:**
A. Gunther asks Paul for help developing the company's new flagship product. He stresses Paul's contribution to the company's improvement.

B. Sara asks William to sit in and contribute to the meetings of a high-powered committee.

C. Pauline wants Mimi's team to put in extra work and offers new computers to help the team improve efficiency.

D. Jose knows Winston is feeling hassled at work, so he sounds him out before he asks him for help.

**Targets:**
1. Task-related
2. Career-related
3. Relationship-related
4. Inspiration-related

**Answer**

Pauline offers a task-related trade object here – namely, a new resource that will help the team get their work done.

Sara uses a career-related trade object to influence William by giving him access to information and contacts, and inclusion in important decisions, planning, and events, thereby boosting his status.

Jose uses a relationship-related trade object by offering understanding and sympathy, and really listening to Winston. Because of this, Winston may be more positive about taking on work.

Gunther uses an inspiration-related trade object. He inspires Paul by emphasizing the significance of the job, and explaining how he can be a part of making it happen.

# SECTION 3 - DETERMINING YOUR TRADING APPROACH TO GET RESULTS

**Section 3 - Determining Your Trading Approach to Get Results**

Reciprocal trading is vital to getting results in everyday business life, especially when you don't have direct authority.

Different trading approaches may be applied in different situations. These approaches included direct trading, demonstrating how cooperation will help a person reach goals, showing hidden value, defraying the costs, and offering flexible compensation.

# TYPES OF TRADING APPROACHES

**Types of trading approaches**
Since the dawn of civilization, people have traded one thing to get another. Whether it's a stone implement or fundamental organizational change you're after, it helps to know the many forms that reciprocity takes. Trades can be complex due to the number of currencies or trade objects used – there are dozens of ways to be paid back.

But if you know the other party's interests and needs, and are aware of the type of relationship you have with the person, you can find an appropriate way to make a trade. Given these factors, there are several approaches you can take to trading:
- make a direct trade for trade items of equivalent value,
- demonstrate how cooperating will help everyone reach goals for your mutual benefit,
- show hidden value when the mutual benefits are not readily apparent,
- defray the costs that arise from your trade, and

- offer flexible compensation when you can't offer immediate payment for a trade.

**Make a direct trade**

A direct trade usually involves two parties with a good level of trust. The key to this trade is that the trade objects are of equal value – the type of objects may vary greatly – for example time, effort, and resources.

**Demonstrate how cooperating will help reach goals**

You can demonstrate how cooperating with a request will help everyone achieve their goals. In order for this to work, you need to convincingly show that your trade will deliver a credible payoff.

**Show hidden value**

Showing hidden value in a trade is an approach you can use when the mutual benefits of your request are not immediately apparent. This usually requires creative thinking and planning to find the unexpected benefits.

**Defray the costs**

You defray the costs when it's hard to find a benefit for others involved in your trade. You present them with the costs involved and find a way to compensate them.

**Offer flexible compensation**

Flexible compensation covers those trades in which you need to postpone compensation. Either you haven't forged a suitable relationship with your trading partners yet, or are unable to obtain a suitable payback for them at the time of trade. In these cases you need to arrange a future payment.

# MAKING A DIRECT TRADE

**Making a direct trade**

The direct trade is the simplest and most easily recognized form of reciprocity. Trading two objects of perceived equal value is the basis of financial markets everywhere, and even happens when you go into your local store and purchase a loaf of bread! Take the example of Amrit and Bruce – they're colleagues at a marketing firm and Amrit needs to ask Bruce a favor.

Amrit and Bruce are peers in a marketing department. Follow along as Amrit approached Bruce to ask him for a favor.

**Amrit:** I was wondering if you'd like to make a small trade.

**Bruce:** What do you have in mind?

**Amrit:** I need to write one more advertising piece for this brochure by tomorrow, but I've just been given an additional assignment. I'll have to work until midnight to finish both projects.

**Bruce:** When's the piece due?

**Amrit:** Nine o'clock tomorrow morning. It'll take about three hours to write. I know you have some downtime now so I thought I would ask.

**Bruce:** That's true. I do have some time.

**Amrit:** And tomorrow afternoon, when things are slow for me, I can review the proposal you're working on for the new client. That will take a couple of hours of my time but that's fair enough.

**Bruce:** Sounds good to me.

Amrit's request is the perfect example of a direct trade. She needed a favor from Bruce and he decided that her offer to review his proposal was worth the extra work. In this trade, both parties deemed the trade objects to be of equivalent value.

Having an established working relationship helps with direct trades because trust exists between the two parties.

But a direct trade can also work when there is no prior relationship between the two parties as long as they both view the trade as equivalent.

A direct trade may require careful thought to show how your request meets the needs of the other party. So it's important to know the other side's needs and interests.

# THE BENEFITS OF COOPERATION

**The benefits of cooperation**

Another approach to trading is to demonstrate how cooperating will help the other person achieve goals. Suppose Bruce isn't interested in Amrit's offer to review his proposal. Amrit now needs to come up with a creative trade object to exchange for Bruce's help with the advertising copy. She decides to demonstrate how cooperating with her request will help Bruce reach his other goals.

Amrit has already asked Bruce to write the advertising copy. Now follow along as Amrit tries to determine a goal for Bruce to reach.

**Bruce:** When's the piece due?

**Amrit:** Nine o'clock tomorrow morning. It'll take about three hours to write. I thought you may be able to use it for your portfolio.

**Bruce:** Yes, thanks Amrit. I'm always looking for a chance to get in some extra writing experience and extra examples for my portfolio!

**Amrit:** That's why I asked you, Bruce.

This type of trade works when both parties benefit from a single action. Amrit benefited by getting Bruce to help with her work and Bruce benefited by doing the work which will add to his portfolio.

**Question**

Which trades demonstrate how cooperating will help a person reach goals?

**Options:**

1. You ask a colleague to handle a report for you and promise to cover work for her in the immediate future

2. You ask for a colleague's help researching a subject, pointing out she'll soon be writing an exam

3. You ask a colleague to help you collate some research for you and, in return, offer to drive him to the airport on your day off

4. You ask a technician in the IT Department to help fix a software bug on your laptop, stressing this will gain him the experience he wants in troubleshooting bugs

**Answer**

Option 1: This option is incorrect. This is an example of flexible compensation where one trade object is exchanged for the promise of future reciprocation.

Option 2: This is a correct option. If your colleague helps with your research, you'll benefit by gaining time and she'll benefit by the extra exposure to the subject for her exam.

Option 3: This option is incorrect. Exchanging the time and effort for collating reports for the time and effort involved in a trip to the airport is an example of a direct trade.

### Getting Results without Direct Authority

Option 4: This is a correct option. The benefit of your request is that the IT technician will gain more experience in an area in which he's interested.

# SHOWING HIDDEN VALUE

**Showing hidden value**

When there's no apparent mutual gain in an exchange, it's necessary to look for hidden value. Often situations have unexpected benefits that can be used to facilitate trades.

Perhaps in your answer to how Amrit should approach the situation, you decide she should find out what will make her request more appealing for Bruce. She needs to find the currency for a direct trade and motivate Bruce to write the advertising copy. Her research reveals that Bruce may be able to use the piece for a paper he's writing for an after-hours course. Bruce is only too happy to help once he realizes he'll benefit from doing the favor for Amrit.

In some situations, the mutual benefits can take effort to discover. But in most cases, you'll be able to pinpoint some hidden value.

For example, if the manager of a production line wants approval to introduce new technology to her area, she might show how the new technology will enable faster turnaround time on lost orders and point to improved customer loyalty as a result.

Focusing on how her request is in the interest of the company, rather than presenting a standard payback analysis on labor savings, she finds hidden value and is persuasive.

# DEFRAYING THE COSTS

**Defraying the costs**

Another approach to a trading situation is to defray – or settle – the costs. You do this when it's not possible to demonstrate your request's benefit. For example, you ask a colleague for a report. You offer to provide a rough draft of it, showing the approach and format to use. This helps reduce the burden of your request for the other party and acts as payment in kind.

**Question**

Which trades demonstrate one party defraying the costs of a request?

**Options:**

1. You ask a manager for a specific assignment and in return he accepts your offer to do some extra administrative work

2. You approach the Accounting Department for some information and prepare special data entry templates to make the bookkeepers' job easier

## Getting Results without Direct Authority

3. You ask your boss to allow you some flexibility in your working hours but also agree to stay late when urgent work needs to get done

4. You ask a colleague to prepare some graphics for a brochure for one of your clients, pointing out that this will help him get more design experience, which he has expressed an interest in

**Answer**

Option 1: This option is incorrect. This is an example of a direct trade in which one trade object is paid for with another of perceived equal value.

Option 2: This option is correct. Before you approach someone with requests for which it's impossible to show the benefits to the other person, you need to acknowledge that costs will be involved and create a plan to compensate the other person for those costs. Here you compensate the bookkeepers for their efforts by making their job easier.

Option 3: This is a correct option. It's important to think about the costs your request might impose and defray those with something. In this case, you are willing to stay late whenever there's urgent work.

Option 4: This option is incorrect. You're demonstrating the benefit of the trade to your colleague in order to secure his cooperation.

# OFFERING FLEXIBLE COMPENSATION

**Offering flexible compensation**

What happens when you wish to trade with colleagues or another organization, but you currently have nothing to offer them? If you don't have an existing relationship, you certainly can't rely on their goodwill, so what do you do?

You offer to pay them back in the future – you offer flexible compensation. Take the example of a freelance programmer who's developing a piece of software. He needs the help of software testers during the entire duration of its development, but lacks the funds to pay for them. He resorts to offering other programmers a testing credit on his software as well as a future payback in time and effort when they need it from him.

**Amrit**

"With this kind of reciprocity, it's necessary to be on good terms with your trading partners. If you're not, what reason would they have to trust you?"

**Bruce**

"Flexible compensation doesn't mean that maybe you'll pay them or maybe you won't. Be sure you can deliver on your promise or your reputation will suffer."

As Amrit and Bruce point out, a trade offering flexible compensation works better if you have a good reputation and people trust you. If you don't, you may have to offer some form of collateral if your trading partners are wary of extending themselves for you with no guarantee of payback.

In the case of the programmer, he has a credible reputation, so his fellow programmers trust him to keep his word. If the trade pays off for everyone involved, his trading partners will be only too eager to make a trade with him in the future.

**Question**

Match each trade approach to the type of example it describes.

**Options:**

A. Direct trade

B. Demonstrate how cooperation will help a person reach goals

C. Defray the costs

D. Show hidden values

E. Offer flexible compensation

**Targets:**

1. You ask a friend to help you and offer something that she considers of equal value in return.

2. You ask a colleague to help you with a project and demonstrate that it will help him achieve his goals.

3. You ask someone for help despite being unable to offer her a trade, so you offer to make the task easier for her.

4. You can't find a trade to offer in exchange for help. You examine the situation and find an unexpected benefit to offer your trading partner.

5. You wish for help from a colleague and offer to pay him back at a future date.

**Answer**

This type of trade involves a direct exchange of trade objects that both parties deem equal in value.

This type of trade involves an exchange in which one party demonstrates how complying with the request will provide benefit for the other party.

This trade involves offering compensation for costs involved in an exchange. These costs can include money, time, effort, and other favors.

Sometimes the mutual benefits of a request or idea may not be immediately apparent so you need to dig deeper to find the value for everyone.

This type of trade involves promising the other party future payment in return for his trade object.

# CHAPTER 4 - INFLUENCING YOUR BOSS

**CHAPTER 4 - Influencing Your Boss**
  Section 1 - Building Influence with Your Boss
  Section 2 - Getting More Responsibility or Direction from Your Boss

# SECTION 1 - BUILDING INFLUENCE WITH YOUR BOSS

**Section 1 - Building Influence with Your Boss**

If you want to have influence over your boss, you have to understand your boss's interests, values, and objectives. To do this, you must first find out about your boss's situation, including responsibilities, relationships with others, and pressures.

You also need to know what you can offer your boss that's beneficial to your work relationship. You should think about valuable trades you can offer based on the resources you control. Finally, you should use a work style that your boss prefers. This will help you be heard.

# THE VALUE OF HAVING INFLUENCE

**The value of having influence**
Being able to build influence with your boss can help you achieve the results you want.

For example, you may want your boss to give you more control over a certain project. If you have effectively developed your relationship, it may be easier for you to achieve this.

Building influence really means establishing an alliance or partnership, which you can do in many ways – for example by showing support, by suggesting answers rather than presenting problems, by knowing what your boss values, and by understanding your boss's work style.

There are two main benefits of being able to build influence with your boss:
- you'll develop a more open work relationship, and
- your boss will be a resource for achievement.

**More open work relationship**
When you develop a more open work relationship, you get to know your boss's values, interests, concerns, and goals. And when you show an understanding of your

boss's situation, your boss is more likely to be open to your ideas and requests.

In addition, your boss may trust you more, feeling that you're understanding and supportive. As a result, your boss will be more open with you and this can help to improve the efficiency of your work.

**A resource for achievement**

When you appropriately develop influence, your boss becomes a resource for achievement, accomplishment, and personal success, rather than the person who's got all the power. When you have influence, you move away from the traditional superior-subordinate relationship and develop more of a partnership with your boss.

Suppose your boss is very demanding and judgmental. You may be inclined to dismiss this type of boss as impossible to work with. But if you assume he's a partner who really wants to succeed and is very worried about failure, then you may be more open to learning from the comments he makes to you.

**Question**

Why is being able to build influence with your boss valuable?

**Options:**

1. You can develop a more open work relationship with your boss

2. You can use your boss as a resource for achievement

3. Your boss will favor you over other employees

4. You'll be able to get more power and then delegate work to your coworkers

**Answer**

Option 1: This option is correct. By building influence with your boss, you're also developing your work relationship. The communication will flow more easily. Your boss will feel much more inclined to listen to your thoughts or ideas if you make it clear that you understand your boss's situation and values.

Option 2: This option is correct. When you seek to build influence with your boss, you move away from the traditional superior-subordinate relationship to more of a partnership with your boss. You view your boss as an ally or partner from whom you can learn.

Option 3: This option is incorrect. Being able to build influence with your boss doesn't necessarily mean you'll become the favorite employee. The key benefits are that you'll develop a more open work relationship and your boss will be a resource for achievement. Your aim should not be to win influence with your boss at the expense of other employees, but rather to work toward your boss's goals, as well as yours.

Option 4: This option is incorrect. Being able to build influence with your boss doesn't give you power over your coworkers. It helps you establish a better working relationship with your boss, who acts as a resource for achievement, rather than a domineering force.

# INFLUENCE AND RELATIONSHIPS

**Influence and relationships**

It may seem strange to think that you can have influence over your boss but you can, and you need to. If you want to achieve your goals, as well as your boss's, you need to build influence with your boss. This means you must take responsibility and make your relationship with your boss a kind of partnership from which you both benefit.

Partners watch out for each other. So you keep each other informed about things you need to know in order to perform your jobs, for example.

In a partnership, you also know what the other person values – and this is key to your gaining influence with your boss.

As you build or maintain the partnership, three techniques can help you obtain influence with your boss:
- make an effort to understand your boss's situation,
- know what you can offer, and
- use a style that your boss prefers.

# UNDERSTAND YOUR BOSS'S SITUATION

**Understand your boss's situation**
You need to consider different aspects of your boss's situation in order to understand the situation fully. Ask yourself questions like "What pressure is my boss under?" and "Who does she report to?" The answers to these questions will help you determine what your boss cares about and values, and you can present your ideas and their benefits in this context.

**Consider aspects of your boss's situation**
When you stop to consider your boss's situation, you may discover things about her that you weren't aware of. You should examine your boss's duties, relationships at work, how she's rewarded or measured, and what internal and external pressures she must deal with.

By taking the time to think about the different parts of your boss's work situation, you may understand better why your boss makes certain decisions or behaves in certain ways.

For example, a financial officer decides not to fulfill a request for the latest technology. Why? Because the officer is measured by certain financial ratios that won't benefit from the addition of expensive equipment that promises no short-term returns.

**Determine what your boss cares about**

Once you've considered your boss's situation, you may have a better idea of her concerns, goals, and values, including which are most important or which are priorities. This is key for determining what to offer to gain cooperation. Influence flows from being able to give people what they need. So the more you know, the better you can determine what your boss needs to achieve her goals, and you'll also know the style in which your boss prefers to interact.

For example, a manager may value people whom she can rely on, who are tough, have the ability to spot good opportunities, and are thorough.

**Present ideas and benefits in context**

Once you know your boss's interests, values, goals, and work style, you're in a better position to show her how a request or idea you have will benefit her.

If you focus on what you want, you can limit the influence you have with your boss. Researching and observing what motivates your boss can help you frame your needs in a way that appeals to her.

Sometimes a good way to understand your boss is to be direct and ask about work issues. Naturally, you may have some fears about doing this, but if you're genuine in your inquiry, it can work well.

## Getting Results without Direct Authority

Your boss may be surprised by – and grateful for – your interest. And it can bring openness and trust into the relationship.

But remember you need to be sincere. If you have a negative view that betrays itself in a loaded question, for example, you may provoke your boss rather than develop your understanding of his situation.

James, a software developer, has realized he doesn't always agree with his boss, Emily. In particular, she seems to want to control his every move – to the point where it feels to him she's his shadow at work. He knows he's not performing at his best and wants to change the way his boss works with him. But first he needs to understand Emily's situation a little better.

He considers the kinds of pressures she faces. He finds out that the group she reports to is very demanding of her and that she's deeply worried about failure. James also knows about the constant deadlines she has to meet.

Drawing on this understanding of her situation, James realizes Emily likes employees who work fast and still produce quality work, and employees who're confident and who she can rely on. She also values time – so she can work on general strategies for the team's success.

Keeping Emily's situation in mind, James can now ask her to give him some leeway in the way he works. But he needs to show confidence and give her something she values in return – quality work done at good speed and a reliable employee.

**Question**

Ayana wants to have more of an influence when introducing new ideas to her boss, Todd. The first thing she has to do is get a good idea of her boss's situation.

How can Ayana get a better understanding of her boss's situation?

**Options:**

1. By considering who Todd reports to and what they're like
2. By finding out what his highest priorities are
3. By asking Todd directly what it is that he's most concerned about
4. By insisting that Todd gives her some of his work so that she understands his situation
5. By focusing on what she needs from Todd and how she can get it

**Answer**

Option 1: This option is correct. Asking questions about Todd's situation helps Ayana clarify what pressures he's under and what's important to him.

Option 2: This is a correct option. Determining Todd's priorities will help Ayana figure out how she can best help him and thereby win some influence with Todd.

Option 3: This option is correct. Taking a direct approach can work when Ayana is genuine and sincere about getting a better understanding of what Todd values.

Option 4: This is an incorrect option. Ayana should observe Todd or ask him directly about his situation rather than taking on his work. This may not be an appropriate approach and could cause Todd to take offense.

Option 5: This option is incorrect. The focus at this point is on finding out about Todd's situation. When Ayana knows what his interests, objectives, and values are, she'll be able to present her new ideas in a way that appeals to him.

# KNOW WHAT YOU CAN OFFER

**Know what you can offer**

In addition to understanding what factors influence how your boss works, you need to know what resources you control that you can offer your boss. In other words, what do you have that could be of value to your boss in a particular situation?

What does your boss need?

Every boss has unique interests, but most bosses welcome it if employees:
- perform above and beyond what's required,
- act as a sounding board for them,
- are a reliable source of information,
- keep them informed of problems - represent them accurately,
- are a source of new ideas,
- support their decisions,
- are encouraging.

You may think that offering quality work on time and keeping out of trouble are enough to offer any boss.

But this may limit your influence. Many employees uncover their boss's main needs and then find a way to meet them. But by doing so, they may be ignoring other types of value they can offer – for example, putting in more than is required or acting as a reliable sounding board for their boss.

Knowing other "valuables" you can offer allows you to link your requests with your boss's goals or build credits that you can exchange for what you want. So it's important to think about what you can control that could be of value to your boss.

Remember James, who wanted his boss Emily to take a less controlling approach? After finding out more about Emily's situation, James asks Emily for more independence in his work. But what can he offer her in return?

In return, James will give her the support to enable her to work more efficiently. She won't have to check up on him at every step, which takes up a lot of her valuable time.

And he'll take ownership of the work, including responsibility for solving any problems.

He'll then present his solutions or completed work to her for review. James assures her that if she discovers any problems with his work, he's willing to stay late to resolve them. This will ultimately give her more time and allow him to work more independently and efficiently.

After he thought about Emily's situation, James realizes he can give Emily the time she values.

And by offering to take ownership of his work and to put in extra time if needed, James removes Emily's worries about his work responsibilities and keeps her informed of problems.

Any boss, including yours, will value these type of actions.

**Question**

Which example best demonstrates how to develop influence by knowing what to offer your boss?

**Options:**

1. Sandra considers her boss's two main needs and determines how to meet them

2. Sandra considers what she controls that would be of value to her boss, including how she can take initiative with new ideas

3. Sandra focuses on her own goals and needs and how fulfilling those might result in something valuable for her boss

**Answer**

Option 1: This option is incorrect. This approach can limit Sandra's influence. When she's aligned with her boss's interests and goals, she'll look beyond his main needs to find other valuable things to offer.

Option 2: This is the correct option. Examining the things Sandra controls that may be of interest to her boss will ultimately allow her to link her requests with her boss's goals. And she builds credits that she can exchange for what she wants.

Option 3: This is an incorrect option. Knowing what to offer her boss means finding out what resources Sandra has that will be of value to him.

# USE STYLE YOUR BOSS PREFERS

**Use style your boss prefers**

Your preferred work style may not always coincide with that of your bosses. A key part of developing influence with your boss is to accommodate to her style.

For example, if your boss doesn't respond well to employees who are too forceful, you may want to take a slightly more deferential approach.

What work style does your boss prefer? It helps to observe your boss and consider, for example, whether he prefers a highly structured schedule or interactions, or likes a more impromptu, spontaneous manner. Knowing this helps you determine how often – and when – to meet and how to present your ideas or requests. The better you understand your boss's preferences, the better you'll work with him.

And knowing your boss's work style will help you get his attention when you need it to achieve your own goals.

A wrong approach or style could mean that your boss doesn't listen carefully to you and you won't be able to influence him.

James approaches Emily with a new idea. He takes a while to introduce it and Emily loses interest before she even hears his idea. She says she has to go because of deadlines. James should have taken Emily's work style into consideration before presenting his idea. She prefers employees who get to the point – she's very no-nonsense and tends to be blunt, even gruff.

**Question**

Which example best demonstrates how to use an appropriate style with your boss?

**Options:**

1. Joan observes her boss to see how he reacts to a forceful approach from someone

2. Joan finds out whether her boss prefers to have all the details or just an outline before making a decision

3. Joan takes a deferential approach with her boss because she's the subordinate

4. Joan presses her boss about an unimportant issue to find out how he reacts under pressure

**Answer**

Option 1: This is a correct option. Observing how Joan's boss responds to different styles will help her determine how best to approach him.

Option 2: This option is correct. Some bosses want all the details, whereas others want an outline of the key points. Joan needs to know which style her boss prefers to get his attention.

Option 3: This option is incorrect. It's important that Joan takes an approach that appeals to her boss, rather than one she thinks suits the traditional employee-boss relationship. Joan's boss may tune out a deferential approach, in which case she won't be able to have much influence with him.

Option 4: This is an incorrect option. Pressing her boss to find out how he reacts is not a good idea. It's better to observe him when someone else is being forceful and take notes on how he reacts.

# SECTION 2 - GETTING MORE RESPONSIBILITY OR DIRECTION FROM YOUR BOSS

**Section 2 - Getting More Responsibility or Direction from Your Boss**

Asking for additional responsibility or direction can be a daunting task, but you need to be able to do it effectively.

To influence your boss to give you the responsibility or direction you seek, you can follow four steps – set aside time to talk to your boss; assess what it is you want and make a specific request; describe how you will accomplish your task or what type of direction you require; and point out the benefits to your boss if the request is granted.

# ASKING FOR MORE RESPONSIBILITY

**Asking for more responsibility**

# MAKING A SPECIFIC REQUEST

## Making a specific request

# DESCRIBING A PLAN

**Describing a plan**

# DESCRIBING THE BENEFITS

**Describing the benefits**

# GLOSSARY

**Glossary**
   **C**
   **confidentiality** - Privacy, as of information that should be kept secret.
   **credibility** - The extent to which a person, idea, or claim can be believed by others.
   **currency** - Credit or good will that you build up with a person by providing them with trade objects they want or need, which may then be redeemed for something you want or need.
   **D**
   **disclaimer** - A word or phrase which distances the speaker from the view expressed.
   **E**
   **expertise** - Skills and knowledge in a particular field.
   **F**
   formal authority - Authority, or influence over others, derived from one's position in a formal organizational structure. For example, people inmanagement positions have formal authority over others.

**G**
**give-and-take** - The concept of reciprocity, stating that, to influence someone to do something for you, you need to do something for them, or give them something they value.

**I**
**influence** - The capacity to persuade others to agree with or support a given point of view, idea, or course of action.

**intensifier** - A word or phrase which hypes up or intensifies the word it refers to.

**M**
**manipulation** - The act of using other people for one's own personal gain, with little or no benefit to them.

**N**
**negotiate** - The act of exchanging viewpoints or ideas as part of the process of finding a mutually beneficial solution or outcome.

**P**
**persuasive communication** - Communication which is believable and wins support for that being communicated.

**Q**
**qualifier** - A word or phrase which puts conditions on or curtails what is being said.

**T**
**trade object** - Something of value (be it an object, a service, assistance, a favor etc.) that can be traded with another person for something you want or need.

# REFERENCES

**References**
1. **The Influence Edge: How to Persuade Others to Help You Achieve Your Goals** - 2000, Alan A. Vengel, Berrett-Koehler Publishers
2. **Influence Without Authority, Second Edition** - 2005, Allan R. Cohen and David L. Bradford, John Wiley & Sons
3. **Power, Influence, and Persuasion: Sell Your Ideas and Make Things Happen** - 2005, Harvard Business School Press, Harvard Business Press
4. **675 Ways to Develop Yourself and Your People: Strategies, Ideas, and Activities for Self-Development and Learning in the Workplace** - 2007, Laurel Alexander, HRD Press
5. **Results Without Authority: Controlling a Project When the Team Doesn't Report to You** - 2006, Tom Kendrick, AMACOM

6. **Exercising Influence: A Guide For Making Things Happen at Work, at Home, and in Your Community, Revised Edition** - 2007, B. Kim Barnes, Pfeiffer
7. **Move the World: Persuade Your Audience, Change Minds, and Achieve Your Goals** - 2007, Dean M. Brenner, John Wiley & Sons
8. **Artful Persuasion: How to Command Attention, Change Minds, and Influence People** - 2000, Harry Mills, AMACOM
9. **Covert Persuasion: Psychological Tactics and Tricks to Win the Game** - 2006, Kevin Hogan and James Speakman, John Wiley & Sons
10. **PeopleSmart: Developing Your Interpersonal Intelligence** - 2000, Mel Silberman, Ph.D. and Freda Hansburg, Ph.D., Berrett-Koehler Publishers
11. **The Influence Edge: How to Persuade Others to Help You Achieve Your Goals** - 2000, Alan A. Vengel, Berrett-Koehler Publishers
12. **100 Ways to Get on the Wrong Side of Your Boss (And Strategies to Prevent You from Getting There!), First Edition** - 2006, Peter R. Garber, Multi-Media Publications Inc.
13. **Managing Your Career For Dummies** - 2000, Max Messmer, John Wiley & Sons

www.ingramcontent.com/pod-product-compliance
Lightning Source LLC
Chambersburg PA
CBHW020914180526
45163CB00007B/2735